Beyond the Report Card

Beyond the Report Card

The Essential Skills for Life That Schools Ignore

Evelyn Hawthorne

Mindful Pages

Published in 2025

ISBN: 9789371777773 (PB)
ISBN: 9789371777841 (eBook)

Published by

Mindful Pages
Imprint of Alpha Editions LLC
312 W. 2nd St #1834
Casper, WY 82601, USA

This book was developed using advanced writing tools to support the drafting and ideation process. All content has been thoughtfully curated, refined, and reviewed to ensure quality and relevance.

Content

Introduction
The Real Curriculum Gap

On a grey spring morning in London, a young graduate sat across from a recruiter, her transcript immaculate, her degree gleaming with distinction. She had spent nearly two decades perfecting the art of school: high marks, polished essays, flawless recall. Yet, when the interviewer asked her how she would manage an unfamiliar budget, or how she might approach a team fractured by conflict, her voice faltered. She knew the quadratic formula. She could recite Shakespeare's soliloquies. But in that moment—when life's messier, unscripted demands appeared—she realised she had been trained for a world that existed mainly on paper.

This scene is not unusual. Every year, tens of thousands of young people step out of classrooms carrying certificates that declare them "prepared." They can demonstrate mastery over syllabi, quote dates and definitions, manipulate algebraic expressions. Yet when faced with the raw uncertainties of adulthood—managing money, reading a room, withstanding stress, making decisions without complete information—they discover that the syllabus stopped short. They are not illiterate, not ignorant, not lazy. They are simply under-prepared in ways no report card ever measured.

Here lies the paradox of modern education: the more precisely we measure academic achievement, the less certain we become that those measurements mean anything beyond the school gates. Grades capture diligence, yes, but they cannot predict whether someone will avoid a predatory loan, recover from failure, discern truth from falsehood online, or sustain healthy relationships. The metrics are clean. Life is not. The result is a curriculum gap—an unspoken, unaddressed chasm between what is taught and what is required.

A Legacy of Measured Knowledge

The modern school was born from the needs of industrial societies. Factories demanded punctuality, obedience, and the capacity to follow rules. Schools responded with rigid timetables, uniform curricula, and an obsession with examinations. In the nineteenth century, as bureaucracies expanded, standardised tests became the efficient tool to sort and rank. By the twentieth, the report card had achieved the status of sacred text: a condensed narrative of a child's potential.

Yet the very qualities rewarded in this system—memorisation, compliance, deference to authority—are those least rewarded by the world beyond it. The labour market no longer demands clerks copying ledgers by hand. It demands creativity, resilience, and judgment under uncertainty. The civic sphere does not need passive absorbers of information; it requires citizens who can weigh conflicting claims, manage collective tension, and see beyond their own echo chambers. The irony is sharp: the longer we hold on to old measures of achievement, the less they serve the needs of the present.

It is tempting to dismiss this as a contemporary complaint, but even earlier thinkers recognised the gap. John Dewey, the American philosopher of education, warned over a century ago that schools risked producing people trained for "recitation" rather than life. What has changed is the scale of the mismatch. Never before have students emerged into a world so saturated with financial complexity, digital distraction, and social fragmentation. The gap has widened into a gulf.

The Stakes of Neglect

This gulf is not abstract. It shows up in statistics that ought to unsettle us. In Britain, nearly half of young adults carry significant consumer debt within just a few years of leaving school. In the United States, student loans have ballooned into a crisis affecting tens of millions. Globally, mental health disorders—anxiety, depression, burnout—are rising fastest among the young. And while social media has given every student a megaphone, it has also eroded their capacity to listen, negotiate, and sustain attention.

These are not failings of individuals. They are systemic omissions. We hand students calculators but never teach them compound interest. We correct their grammar but rarely help them detect manipulation in a newsfeed. We penalise them for failing tests but seldom show them how to fail constructively in life. To imagine that the grade is a proxy for preparedness is to confuse the map with the terrain.

If anything, the terrain has become rougher. Globalisation and digitalisation have shredded the idea of stable careers. Automation has unsettled traditional professions. Political polarisation has intensified the need for critical discernment. The climate crisis confronts the next generation with decisions of extraordinary complexity. To step into this world with nothing but grades as armour is like sending sailors into stormy seas with a manual of knots but no experience of waves.

Beyond the Binary of "Soft" and "Hard" Skills

Critiques of education often veer into nostalgia—lamenting a lost golden age, or exalting vaguely defined "soft skills" as the antidote. This book takes a different route. It does not pit algebra against empathy, nor suggest that Shakespeare is irrelevant to survival. Rather, it insists that what we call "soft" skills—resilience, financial literacy, social intelligence, emotional regulation—are not optional extras but the very architecture of adult competence. They are not soft; they are structural.

Consider resilience: the ability to recover from setbacks, to interpret failure as feedback, to endure difficulty without collapse. Or consider financial literacy: the knowledge not merely of earning but of managing, saving, and investing. These are not luxuries. They are survival tools. Yet they are absent from most curricula, treated as extracurricular, left to chance or family circumstance. This neglect perpetuates inequality, since those whose parents or communities model these skills thrive, while others stumble without guidance.

The binary itself—between academic rigour and life competence—is a false one. A truly future-proof education would integrate both: the intellectual depth to analyse, and the practical wisdom to act.

A Framework for the Unspoken Syllabus

This book aims to articulate what schools leave unsaid. It maps the skills that, while rarely tested, shape the trajectory of a life. Money management. Emotional literacy. Critical thinking in a digital fog. Resilience in the face of failure. Social navigation in diverse contexts. Attention in a world that commodifies distraction. Decision-making under uncertainty. And finally, a redefinition of success fit for the twenty-first century.

Each chapter takes one domain and interrogates it with evidence, history, and practical insight. You will encounter research from psychology and behavioural economics, stories from individuals who have succeeded despite traditional markers, and habits that can be cultivated in daily life. The aim is neither utopian nor defeatist. It is pragmatic: to equip readers with the tools schools forgot to teach.

A recurring motif will guide us: the idea of "future-proofing." In engineering, to future-proof is to design something not for current conditions but for those yet to come. Likewise, the skills explored here are not relics of the past but investments in adaptability. They are not about securing one perfect outcome but about navigating shifting terrain with clarity and courage.

The Urgency and the Invitation

Why does this matter now? Because the gap between what is taught and what is needed is no longer tolerable background noise. It is becoming the defining crisis of education. We cannot afford to treat adulthood as a crash course delivered after the fact. Nor can we continue outsourcing essential knowledge to luck, family background, or the occasional inspiring mentor. To thrive in a world of flux, every student deserves a framework that prepares them not just to answer questions, but to ask better ones; not just to recite facts, but to exercise judgment.

This book is an invitation—to parents, educators, policymakers, and above all, to learners themselves. It is not an indictment of teachers, who work within constraints they did not design. Nor is it a rejection of knowledge, which remains indispensable. It is, instead, a call to widen the frame: to measure success not by grades alone but by the skills that carry us when the syllabus runs out.

What does it mean to be educated if you cannot manage your own money? If you collapse under the first stress of failure? If you cannot distinguish fact from fiction in a feed of headlines? If you mistake attention for multitasking, or ambition for burnout? These are not rhetorical flourishes. They are the questions every graduate now faces, whether or not the exam board prepared them.

Looking Ahead

The chapters that follow do not merely critique; they construct. They expose the illusions of A+ thinking, chart the terrain of financial literacy, unravel the unspoken language of emotion, and confront the challenges of thinking clearly in an age of noise. They explore resilience not as a slogan but as a discipline, social navigation not as etiquette but as survival, attention not as a luxury but as a currency, and decision-making not as guesswork but as craft. They culminate in a redefinition of success, one that does not discard ambition but anchors it in sustainability and freedom.

To step beyond the report card is to step into life as it is: unpredictable, demanding, full of noise and possibility. The question is not whether we will face complexity. We will. The question is whether we will enter it blind, armed only with grades, or equipped with the deeper skills that make adulthood not merely survivable but meaningful.

The real curriculum gap is vast, but it is not insurmountable. What follows is a map—not perfect, not final, but necessary. Let us begin.

Chapter 1
The Hidden Cost of A+ Thinking

At first glance, the photograph is triumphant: a teenager in a cap and gown, arms raised, diploma aloft, the crowd applauding as though a finish line has been crossed. It is the kind of image that fills family albums and school prospectuses alike, a distilled promise of success. Yet look a little closer—beyond the ceremony, beyond the polished stage—and you find the quieter aftermath: graduates stepping into adulthood armed with test scores but uncertain about mortgages, degrees but uneasy about mental health, gold medals in academic compliance but silver skills in resilience and judgment. The illusion is seductive. Education has persuaded us that high marks equate to preparedness. But when the applause fades, the mismatch between academic success and adult competence comes sharply into focus.

Consider the young professional who soared through university but finds herself paralysed by her first serious financial decision: whether to take on a mortgage with fluctuating interest rates. Or the graduate who aced every exam but falters when confronting conflict in the workplace, unsure how to mediate tension or read unspoken cues. These are not failures of intelligence. They are the inevitable results of a system that equates preparation with performance on paper, and neglects the deeper competencies that real life demands.

This chapter confronts that paradox. Schools claim to prepare students for the "real world," but the world they rehearse belongs largely to the classroom: one of right answers, predictable rules, and neat rubrics. Outside those walls, decisions are riddled with ambiguity, challenges come without warning, and success requires more than the capacity to memorise. Yet still, the report card reigns supreme, its letters and numbers shaping futures with a confidence they scarcely deserve.

The obsession with grades has a long lineage. In the nineteenth century, as nation-states industrialised, standardised testing emerged as an efficient way to sort citizens into bureaucracies, armies, and factories. By the twentieth, the A+ had become a badge of honour, shorthand for intelligence and diligence. Employers trusted it. Parents aspired to it. Students built their identities around it. It seemed rational: what better predictor of future excellence than past excellence measured consistently?

But what if that very measurement distorts our understanding of success? Research has repeatedly shown that while high grades may predict further academic progression, they are poor predictors of life satisfaction, career adaptability, or financial stability. Many of history's most influential figures were mediocre students, while some of the brightest exam-takers vanish into obscurity, paralysed by perfectionism or undone by the first setback ungraded by a teacher. The correlation is weak because the skill sets are different. School rewards accuracy; life rewards adaptability. The classroom punishes mistakes; the world often requires them as a precondition for growth.

The cost of clinging to outdated metrics is not only individual but societal. By privileging what can be easily measured, education systems neglect what is essential but difficult to quantify: judgment, empathy, resilience, imagination. These qualities shape leaders, innovators, and citizens, yet they rarely appear on a transcript. And when schools do venture into broader competencies—teamwork projects, "life skills" workshops—they are too often marginal, squeezed to the periphery by the gravitational pull of examinations.

Curriculum design is equally culpable. While technology, finance, and culture evolve at breakneck speed, school syllabi often change at a glacial pace. Students graduate into a digital economy with barely a lesson on algorithms, into a consumer society with no formal grounding in budgeting, into a mental health crisis with scant tools for emotional regulation. It is not that educators are blind to these realities. It is that institutions resist volatility. To adapt curricula swiftly is to admit that knowledge itself is provisional. Yet life has already taught us that truth. The world students inherit is provisional, shifting, unfinished.

This reluctance leaves young people vulnerable. They emerge fluent in Shakespeare yet illiterate in credit contracts, versed in quadratic equations yet bewildered by the logic of compound interest, capable of parsing poetry but incapable of parsing the emotional signals that govern relationships and workplaces. These are not trivial deficits. They are the very conditions of adult life. The result is a generation praised for achievement yet anxious about survival.

Why, then, do the old metrics persist? The answer lies partly in convenience. Grades and test scores offer a crisp hierarchy, simple enough to digest and efficient for institutions to administer. They provide parents with reassurance, universities with filters, and governments with data points. But beneath the surface, they obscure as much as they reveal. They reduce intelligence to compliance, learning to memorisation, and potential to a number. It is as though we have mistaken the shadows on the wall for reality, trusting the exam hall's flickering light instead of stepping outside into the messy sunlight of lived experience.

Yet cracks in this edifice are widening. Employers increasingly voice frustration that graduates, though credentialled, lack initiative and adaptability. Psychologists warn that perfectionism, fuelled by grade obsession, is linked to rising anxiety and burnout. Economists note that societies with rigid credential systems risk stifling entrepreneurship. Even parents, once proud of their children's top marks, question why these marks do not translate into resilience or practical wisdom. The A+ is becoming a hollow accolade—shiny but fragile, prestigious but costly.

This chapter unpacks these contradictions. We will begin with *the illusion of preparation*, examining how the rituals of schooling reward obedience and recall rather than the judgment required in a complex world. We will then turn to *grades versus life outcomes*, showing how the metrics of success inside the classroom diverge sharply from those that sustain well-being and resilience outside it. Next, we will probe *the blind spot of curriculum design*, asking why finance, emotions, and decision-making remain neglected despite their centrality to adult life. Finally, we will consider *why the old metrics fail*, tracing how grades and degrees—once useful proxies for intelligence—have ossified into obstacles, preventing us from seeing what truly matters.

The aim is not to disparage academic achievement. Knowledge matters, and intellectual rigour should be defended. But when achievement is conflated with preparedness, when the A+ becomes the sole horizon of aspiration, the cost is borne by the very people it was meant to serve. Students enter adulthood believing they are equipped, only to discover that the tools they have mastered are ill-suited to the tasks ahead.

The hidden cost of A+ thinking is not paid in exam halls. It is paid in the quiet panic of the graduate who cannot navigate a lease, in the disillusionment of the worker unmoored by failure, in the collective fragility of a generation trained for certainty but handed uncertainty. These costs are invisible on a transcript but deeply visible in lives.

As we turn the page, consider this: what if the very system designed to prepare us is the one that leaves us least prepared? And what if, by clinging to the safety of familiar metrics, we are sacrificing the skills that would actually help us thrive? These are the questions at the heart of this chapter—and the beginning of a larger reckoning with how we define, pursue, and measure education itself.

The Illusion of Preparation

On paper, the promise is flawless. Schools declare themselves gateways to the future, equipping the young with the knowledge and skills needed to thrive. Teachers hand back assignments stamped with reassuring marks, parents applaud each grade as proof of readiness, and policymakers cite test scores as evidence of national progress. Yet the ritual conceals a disquieting paradox: the very system that proclaims to prepare students often leaves them ill-prepared for the complexity of adult life. Success in the classroom does not reliably translate into competence in the world beyond it. The closer one examines the promise, the more fragile it appears.

Consider the teenager who excels at every examination, admired for her discipline and diligence. She arrives at university brimming with accolades, only to find herself undone by the first experience of real autonomy: budgeting her allowance, negotiating flatmate disputes, resisting the temptations of credit cards. None of these challenges can be solved by memorising a textbook or regurgitating a model answer. They demand judgment, foresight, and emotional balance—

qualities her schooling neither rewarded nor cultivated. The same story repeats across cultures and continents: graduates fluent in abstract concepts, but halting when confronted with unstructured problems, interpersonal tensions, or ethical dilemmas.

The illusion of preparation persists because education has conflated two distinct outcomes: performance under controlled conditions and competence under uncertain ones. The former is easy to measure; the latter is messy, fluid, resistant to neat rubrics. Schools gravitate toward what can be codified and examined, privileging the recall of information over the cultivation of discernment. Compliance—knowing how to satisfy instructions—is rewarded more consistently than curiosity or originality. As long as students deliver what is asked, they are deemed prepared, even if the world outside will rarely present them with tasks framed so clearly.

The gulf is not merely anecdotal. Research in psychology and education demonstrates how academic achievement, measured narrowly by grades, correlates only weakly with later indicators of adult competence such as financial stability, emotional resilience, or career adaptability. Employers frequently lament that graduates, though technically knowledgeable, lack initiative, problem-solving capacity, and the ability to navigate ambiguity. These are not minor shortcomings. They are the very conditions of modern life, in which technological disruption, shifting economies, and volatile politics ensure that uncertainty is the norm. A curriculum designed for stability is, by definition, a curriculum unfit for reality.

History shows that this disjunction has long been noticed, though rarely addressed. Philosophers from Dewey to Whitehead warned against mistaking schooling for education, rote learning for genuine understanding. Yet institutions remain stubbornly loyal to the visible rituals of preparation: the exam hall, the grade sheet, the graduation stage. These are symbols that reassure parents, administrators, and governments, even if they no longer reassure life itself. The rituals persist not because they are effective, but because they are legible. They provide a neat record of progress in a world that hungers for certainty, even when the certainty is spurious.

The cost of this illusion is paid in the vulnerability of students released into adulthood without the mental tools to interpret complexity. Confronted with a world that demands critical discernment, they default to the habits ingrained by schooling: searching for the right answer, deferring to authority, fearing mistakes. Yet life rarely supplies answer keys. Decisions about careers, relationships, finances, or citizenship are riddled with competing truths, shifting probabilities, and irreversible trade-offs. A student who has been rewarded only for perfection finds failure unbearable; one who has been trained only in obedience finds independence terrifying. The system claims to have prepared them. In reality, it has prepared them for an environment that scarcely exists.

Why, then, has education clung so tightly to this model? Part of the answer lies in the seductive clarity of measurement. Grades, test scores, and league tables transform the messy business of learning into digestible numbers. They allow institutions to compare, to rank, to sort. In a bureaucratic age, such clarity is politically and administratively convenient. But clarity can be deceptive. It disguises the fact that what matters most—judgment, resilience, creativity—resists quantification. We measure what is easy, then convince ourselves that what is easy to measure must also be what is important. The illusion is complete when students themselves internalise the same logic, equating self-worth with scores, believing that achievement under exam conditions is sufficient armour against the contingencies of life.

This is not to dismiss the value of knowledge or academic rigour. To know history, mathematics, or literature is to enlarge the mind, to sharpen tools of thought. But when such knowledge is divorced from the contexts in which it will be used, it becomes inert. A graduate may know the theories of supply and demand yet fall prey to high-interest payday loans. A student may recite the stages of cognitive development yet fail to recognise their own anxiety. Knowledge matters, but only when woven into judgment, only when tested against the unpredictable texture of reality.

The illusion of preparation also deepens inequality. Students from affluent families often acquire practical wisdom outside school—

from parents who model financial literacy, emotional regulation, or social negotiation. For others, school may be the only structured environment available. When schools confine themselves to narrow academic metrics, they unwittingly widen the gulf between those who inherit competence at home and those who must construct it without guidance. The system then compounds the inequality by mistaking high marks for merit, ignoring the unmeasured struggles that shape resilience.

The danger of clinging to the illusion is not simply wasted potential, but disillusionment. When students who have excelled academically encounter the chaos of adult life and find themselves floundering, they often turn their disappointment inward, mistaking systemic omission for personal failure. They believe they must be deficient because, despite their A grades, they cannot manage debt, sustain focus, or recover from setbacks. In truth, it is the system that failed them, by rewarding the shallow simulacrum of preparation rather than its substance.

And so we are left with a paradox: a system that insists it equips students for life while consistently neglecting the very qualities life demands. The contradiction is stark enough to provoke uncomfortable questions. If the rituals of schooling prepare students only for more schooling, who will prepare them for life? If judgment, resilience, and adaptability are learned mostly by accident or privilege, what becomes of those who lack both? If society continues to mistake compliance for competence, how many crises—financial, social, political—must be endured before the illusion is finally abandoned?

The answers are not simple, nor are they contained within the boundaries of traditional curricula. But recognising the illusion is the first step toward piercing it. The promise of preparation cannot remain a performance staged within exam halls; it must become a lived reality tested against the complexity of the world itself. Until then, the applause of graduation ceremonies will continue to echo hollowly against the silence of unprepared lives.

Grades vs. Life Outcomes

At Harvard University, researchers once conducted a long-term study tracking students from their first-year dormitories through to late adulthood. Many of those who arrived with impeccable transcripts—straight A students, prizes in Latin, mathematics prodigies—were not the ones who went on to live the longest, happiest, or most resilient lives. Some excelled only in their twenties and thirties, faltering when faced with divorce, financial shocks, or health crises. Others, whose grades had been modest, proved to be the steady achievers: building fulfilling careers, sustaining relationships, navigating uncertainty with composure. The paradox was stark. The system's top performers did not necessarily become life's most successful players.

We find versions of this paradox everywhere. The "class genius" who dazzled with perfect recall is now restless in midlife, struggling to reinvent a career in an economy that demands adaptability more than mastery of a single domain. The diligent student who aced every exam enters a prestigious firm only to burn out within a few years, unable to withstand the relentless pace. Meanwhile, a former B-student, once dismissed as average, thrives as an entrepreneur—resilient, resourceful, and capable of turning uncertainty into opportunity. Grades tell us much about academic aptitude, but strikingly little about who will flourish when life refuses to follow the syllabus.

This disconnect is not simply anecdotal but documented in research across decades. Psychologists studying predictors of life satisfaction consistently find that academic achievement explains only a sliver of variance in adult well-being. The Harvard Study of Adult Development, one of the longest-running longitudinal studies in the world, shows that the strongest predictors of happiness and health are not grades, nor even intelligence, but the quality of relationships and the capacity for emotional regulation. Economists examining financial resilience point to traits such as delayed gratification, adaptability, and problem-solving as stronger indicators of stability than any exam score. The evidence converges on a blunt truth:

grades open doors, but they do not teach us how to walk through them.

The structure of schooling helps explain why. Grades reward accuracy, conformity to expectations, and mastery of narrow domains under controlled conditions. Real life, by contrast, rewards adaptability, judgement, and the ability to act under uncertainty. A student may learn to derive the quadratic formula but never be taught how to navigate a layoff, how to negotiate a contract, or how to detect predatory lending. Life's problems arrive without rubrics. They rarely offer the clarity of "correct" versus "incorrect." Instead, they demand discernment amidst ambiguity. In such conditions, academic training provides only partial preparation.

One of the most striking examples of this mismatch is found in the workplace. Surveys of employers routinely report frustration that graduates, while technically competent, lack initiative, communication skills, and resilience. The World Economic Forum ranks critical thinking, complex problem-solving, and adaptability among the top skills needed for the 21st century—none of which can be adequately captured by a GPA. Indeed, some of the most valuable professional traits—such as the ability to recover after failure, or to maintain composure during conflict—are actively undermined by schooling's obsession with perfection. If you have been rewarded only for flawless performance, how do you cope when perfection is impossible?

The consequences are visible in mental health statistics. Rising rates of anxiety and depression among high-achieving students suggest that grades, far from guaranteeing stability, can cultivate fragility. The pressure to maintain top marks trains young people to fear mistakes, to equate self-worth with performance. This mindset proves disastrous in adulthood, where mistakes are inevitable and recovery is essential. The straight-A student may carry into adulthood an intolerance of failure, while the middling student, accustomed to setbacks, may develop resilience almost by accident. It is not the grade itself that matters but the habits and attitudes forged in its pursuit.

Philosophically, the problem is older than modern education. Aristotle distinguished between *episteme*—theoretical knowledge—and *phronesis*—practical wisdom. Schools privilege the former, assuming that knowledge will translate into competence. Yet life repeatedly demonstrates that *phronesis* is indispensable: the ability to deliberate well about the things that matter, to choose wisely in conditions of uncertainty. To measure only *episteme* and neglect *phronesis* is to produce lopsided adults, brilliant in abstraction but brittle in practice. The tension between these two kinds of knowledge lies at the heart of the mismatch between grades and outcomes.

There are, of course, counterexamples—high achievers who carry their diligence into adulthood, translating academic discipline into professional excellence. But even here, their success often depends less on the grades themselves than on the traits that underpinned them: perseverance, organisation, a willingness to practise. The grade is a symbol, not a destiny. To mistake it for a guarantee is to confuse a marker with the substance it only partially reflects.

The problem deepens when societies fetishise credentials. Degrees and GPAs become gatekeepers for opportunity, even when they bear little relation to the skills demanded by a role. A talented but average student may be excluded from elite professions, while a high-achiever gains entry but lacks staying power. This produces inefficiency at scale: talent squandered, institutions populated by those skilled in passing tests rather than navigating reality. The illusion of meritocracy persists, but beneath it lies a machinery that mistakes conformity for competence.

Consider the global financial crisis of 2008. The institutions at its heart were filled with graduates of the world's most prestigious universities, all decorated with top grades in economics, finance, and mathematics. Yet these same institutions engineered catastrophic misjudgements, fuelled by overconfidence and herd thinking. The paradox could not be clearer: academic brilliance did not prevent systemic folly. The graduates had mastered equations but overlooked judgement. The consequences reverberated across the world.

If grades cannot predict resilience, happiness, or financial prudence, what should we value instead? The answer is not to discard knowledge or diminish intellectual rigour, but to broaden our conception of what counts as success. We must learn to prize adaptability, emotional clarity, social intelligence, and critical discernment alongside cognitive achievement. In other words, to supplement the report card with the qualities that life itself will inevitably test.

Yet here lies the difficulty: these qualities are harder to measure. A test can capture recall, but not the capacity to navigate grief. A grade can record accuracy, but not courage under pressure. The invisibility of these traits makes them easy to neglect, yet their absence becomes glaring once students step beyond the classroom.

The challenge for educators, parents, and policymakers is profound. How can we cultivate skills that resist simple quantification? How can we design systems that reward not only compliance but also curiosity, not only correctness but also courage? These questions remain unresolved. What is certain is that the cost of ignoring them is paid daily—in the lives of graduates bewildered by adulthood, in the anxieties of high-achievers who crumble outside controlled conditions, in the wasted potential of those whose modest grades concealed extraordinary capacities.

The paradox remains unresolved and unsettling. If the brightest students on paper are not always the brightest in life, what does it mean to be "educated"? And if the report card is no longer a reliable map of the terrain ahead, what markers should we trust instead? These questions, more than grades themselves, will shape the future of education—and the futures of those who pass through it.

The Blind Spot of Curriculum Design

In 2008, as the global financial system unravelled, commentators were quick to identify reckless lending and speculative excess as the culprits. Less remarked upon was another, subtler cause: millions of ordinary citizens had entered the crisis without even the most basic financial literacy. Many did not understand adjustable-rate mortgages, compound interest, or the long-term consequences of debt. These were not fringe details of adult life; they were the very mechanics of survival in a modern economy. Yet for most, they had never been part of school. It is a striking paradox: institutions that claim to prepare students for life consistently sidestep the domains in which life most relentlessly tests us.

This blind spot is not limited to finance. Emotional regulation—the ability to manage stress, recover from setbacks, and interpret one's inner world—remains largely absent from formal curricula, despite its demonstrable impact on health, relationships, and professional performance. Decision-making, the craft of weighing trade-offs under uncertainty, is treated as though it were an instinct rather than a skill, even though every adult life is structured around consequential choices. Schools continue to focus on teaching trigonometry while leaving students to improvise their way through credit contracts, panic attacks, or career pivots.

Why does this omission persist? Part of the answer lies in inertia. Curricula are conservative by design, often taking years to reform, while culture and economy transform at pace. By the time a new subject is debated, approved, and standardised, the world it sought to address has already shifted. Another part lies in institutional discomfort. Finance, emotions, and decision-making are messy, culturally contested, and politically charged. To teach them demands grappling with values, biases, and the unpredictable diversity of human experience. Schools, seeking neutrality and clarity, retreat instead into the safer territory of established subjects where answers can be neatly graded.

The effect is an educational time lag. Students leave school fluent in knowledge that once signified rigour—Latin declensions, the periodic table, Shakespearean metre—yet unequipped for the complexity of the digital, financial, and psychological landscapes they must navigate. In the meantime, industries of self-help, coaching, and private tutoring rush to fill the void, commodifying the very skills schools decline to teach. The irony is sharp: the public system, ostensibly designed to level opportunity, neglects essential life competencies, while the private market sells them back at a premium.

Consider the example of financial literacy. Studies across multiple countries show that even highly educated adults struggle with basic financial concepts. In the United States, nearly two-thirds of millennials cannot correctly answer simple questions on interest rates or inflation. In the UK, surveys reveal widespread misunderstanding of pensions and credit. The consequences are tangible: higher rates of personal debt, vulnerability to predatory lending, and diminished long-term security. Yet despite repeated calls from economists and policymakers, most school systems continue to treat personal finance as optional enrichment rather than core curriculum.

Emotional regulation is treated with similar neglect. Mental health crises among young people are escalating, with anxiety and depression now among the leading causes of disability worldwide. Research consistently links emotional literacy—the capacity to identify, understand, and manage emotions—to resilience, social connection, and even workplace performance. And yet schools often prioritise disciplinary control over emotional education, rewarding suppression rather than self-awareness. Students are expected to manage stress, yet are rarely given tools to do so. When they fail, we call it weakness, rather than acknowledge it as a systemic omission.

Decision-making, too, is left to chance. In classrooms, problems are framed with clear parameters and right answers, fostering an expectation that choices are tidy and information is complete. But real decisions—whether to change careers, move cities, marry, or invest—are rarely so clean. They require reasoning under uncertainty, an acceptance of risk, and the courage to act without guarantees. These are skills that can be taught, drawing from behavioural science, philosophy, and practical heuristics. Yet they remain absent from curricula, as though adulthood will magically bestow them upon graduation.

There are, of course, reasons for caution. Teaching finance risks appearing partisan if it touches on policy debates about debt or taxation. Teaching emotional regulation risks accusations of overreach into parental or therapeutic domains. Teaching decision-making risks unsettling traditional hierarchies of authority, by encouraging students to question and weigh rather than simply obey.

These anxieties are not unfounded. Yet their cost is higher: a generation of adults stumbling through the most consequential aspects of life unguided.

The irony is that these omitted subjects are not marginal but foundational. Without financial literacy, students risk lifelong debt. Without emotional regulation, they risk burnout and broken relationships. Without decision-making skills, they risk paralysis or reckless choices. These are not "extras" but determinants of whether the knowledge gained in school can be applied meaningfully in life. A doctor who understands biology but cannot regulate stress is a liability. An engineer who masters equations but cannot manage money is vulnerable. A politician versed in history but unable to weigh trade-offs may imperil thousands.

The persistence of this blind spot reflects a deeper philosophical problem: the conflation of education with information. Schools excel at transmitting knowledge, but knowledge alone is insufficient. Competence requires integration—information applied through judgment, tested against lived experience. By neglecting domains that cannot be mastered by memorisation alone, curricula perpetuate a narrow vision of learning that prepares students only for further schooling, not for life.

What, then, should education look like if it were to close this gap? It would not mean abandoning literature, mathematics, or science. These remain vital. But alongside them, curricula would need to embed financial competence, emotional literacy, and decision-making as non-negotiable foundations. Students would leave not only knowing the mechanics of a sonnet or a cell, but also how to read a contract, regulate stress, and weigh uncertain choices. These are the skills that allow knowledge to be lived, rather than merely recalled.

The question is whether societies are willing to make such a shift. Reform is slow, and resistance entrenched. It is easier to measure exam results than resilience, easier to grade algebra than adaptability. Yet the longer we delay, the wider the gap grows between what is taught and what is required. Each cohort graduates into a world moving faster than the one before, carrying knowledge that is partial and leaving school without the skills most predictive of whether they will flourish or falter.

And so the unresolved tension remains: if schools will not teach the competencies most essential to life, who will? Families vary in capacity, workplaces arrive too late, and the marketplace offers uneven, costly substitutes. The silence of curricula on finance, emotions, and decision-making is not a neutral omission—it is an abdication of responsibility. Whether education systems can overcome their own inertia may determine not only the futures of individuals, but the resilience of societies themselves.

Why the Old Metrics Fail

In 1910, a sixteen-year-old boy left school in rural Ohio, having performed poorly in nearly every subject. His teachers had judged him slow, inattentive, even incapable. Within a decade, that boy—Thomas Edison—would transform the modern world with inventions that reshaped light, sound, and communication. His story is repeated in countless variations: the student labelled mediocre who later demonstrates extraordinary vision, and the student decorated with top grades who struggles to adapt once the guardrails of formal schooling disappear. The paradox is enduring: society continues to equate academic marks with intelligence, despite overwhelming evidence that the connection is partial at best.

The reliance on grades, test scores, and degrees as proxies for ability is understandable. They offer clarity in a messy world, a shorthand for employers and institutions seeking to filter vast numbers of applicants. A transcript condenses years of effort into a single number or letter, a degree certificate into a line on a CV. But clarity can be deceptive. Like a photograph that captures a face but misses its voice, these metrics capture only one narrow dimension of intelligence. They reflect diligence, memory, and conformity to instruction, but leave untouched creativity, resilience, and judgment—the very traits that determine long-term flourishing.

Consider the world of work. Employers often insist on degree requirements for roles that bear little relation to academic training.

A university diploma is treated as proof of general competence, yet research repeatedly shows that it predicts job performance only weakly. High test scores may reveal a talent for performing under exam conditions, but they do not ensure adaptability in a turbulent marketplace. As technology automates routine tasks, the premium shifts away from rote knowledge and towards skills that no exam can capture: collaboration, critical thinking, ethical discernment. The credential lingers as a gatekeeper, even as its relevance wanes.

The persistence of these old metrics is not only inefficient but distortive. When grades are treated as destiny, students internalise the belief that a mark on a page defines their capacity. A single poor exam becomes a verdict on intelligence rather than a reflection of circumstance. Conversely, a string of high marks may instil a dangerous complacency, persuading students that success will flow inevitably from their academic prowess. Both narratives are false. Both produce fragility: the underachiever who gives up prematurely, and the high achiever who collapses at the first ungraded setback.

At the cultural level, the obsession with metrics shapes the very design of education. Schools narrow their teaching to what can be tested, often at the expense of what matters most. Creativity is stifled when there is no mark scheme for imagination. Emotional regulation is ignored because it cannot be graded with precision. Decision-making is left to chance because ambiguity defies neat assessment. The old metrics do not simply fail to measure essential skills; they actively crowd them out.

Philosophically, this fixation reflects a deeper error: the conflation of intelligence with knowledge recall. Psychologists from Alfred Binet, the pioneer of IQ testing, to contemporary scholars of multiple intelligences, have argued that human ability is plural, encompassing not only analytical reasoning but also spatial, emotional, and practical capacities. Yet the school report card and university transcript persist in reducing this richness to narrow academic bands. It is a distortion reminiscent of the drunk searching for his keys under the lamppost—not because he lost them there, but because the light is better. We measure where it is easy, not where it is meaningful.

The consequences extend beyond education into society at large. Political leaders, corporate executives, and policymakers are often selected through pathways that privilege academic distinction. Yet history shows that elite credentials do not immunise against poor judgment. The architects of the 2008 financial collapse, many graduates of the world's top universities, were not unintelligent; they were miseducated by a system that prized technical mastery while neglecting prudence, humility, and foresight. Old metrics helped propel them into positions of authority, but those same metrics had failed to capture the qualities necessary to wield authority responsibly.

The tension is particularly visible in our digital age. Standardised tests reward the ability to memorise facts, yet factual recall has never been less valuable. A smartphone can supply dates, definitions, or formulas in seconds. What the device cannot supply is discernment: the ability to sift truth from falsehood, to evaluate competing claims, to apply knowledge ethically. By clinging to outdated proxies, we risk training students for a world that no longer exists, while neglecting the world they actually inhabit—one of information overload, algorithmic manipulation, and ethical complexity.

Some argue that grades and degrees remain useful signals: imperfect but necessary in large-scale systems where employers or universities cannot know every candidate personally. There is truth in this. Metrics provide efficiency. But efficiency is not accuracy. To mistake the signal for the substance is to perpetuate inequities, exclude unconventional talent, and misallocate human potential. Worse, it risks perpetuating a false sense of security: the belief that those with high marks are inherently equipped to lead, decide, and innovate. The illusion is comfortable, but costly.

The question, then, is not whether to measure, but what—and how. If we recognise that the old metrics distort, we must seek frameworks that capture adaptability, resilience, ethical reasoning, and social intelligence. These are harder to quantify, but not impossible to cultivate. Apprenticeships, project-based learning, collaborative problem-solving, and reflective assessment all offer glimpses of alternative models. Yet until they are embraced at scale, grades and degrees will continue to dominate, their inadequacy camouflaged by tradition.

Here lies the unresolved tension. Society needs markers of competence; individuals need validation of their progress. But if those markers are misaligned with the demands of reality, they serve neither. How long can we persist in equating numbers on a page with the fullness of human ability? And what might emerge if, instead of clinging to old proxies, we dared to construct new ones—frameworks designed not for the world of yesterday, but for the world already unfolding before us?

Chapter 2
Money Without a Map

On a rainy afternoon in Manchester, a twenty-two-year-old graduate signed her first rental agreement. She skimmed the fine print, assuming her degree in economics had prepared her to navigate numbers. Three months later, she was drowning in hidden fees, a rent clause that rose unpredictably, and a stack of credit card bills she had relied on to bridge the gap between salary and survival. She had mastered differential equations but not direct debits, game theory but not the grim reality of compound debt. What she had mistaken for competence was, in truth, an illusion—and one that many young adults discover only when it is too late.

Financial illiteracy does not announce itself with dramatic fanfare. It creeps in quietly: the overdraft that becomes permanent, the payday loan taken in desperation, the car bought on terms too complex to decode. By the time its consequences are visible—stress, spiralling interest, long-term insecurity—the damage is already entrenched. The modern economy is unforgiving of ignorance. It punishes mistakes ruthlessly, rewarding those who can navigate its intricacies and preying on those who cannot. And yet, paradoxically, schools—those institutions that claim to prepare young people for the world—rarely teach the basic mechanics of money.

The result is a strange double-bind. We send students into adulthood after years of study, often burdened with debt from the very education that neglected to equip them with financial survival skills. They know how to analyse a Shakespearean sonnet or balance a chemical equation, but they cannot explain the difference between a fixed and variable mortgage rate. They can recall historical timelines yet falter when asked to budget across a single month. Earning may come easily; managing does not. What should be regarded as foundational literacy is treated instead as optional enrichment, left to chance, family background, or private trial and error.

This omission is not trivial. The ability to earn money and the ability to manage it are distinct, and the gulf between them can define a life. Many young professionals step into promising careers only to find their earnings evaporate under the weight of lifestyle inflation, impulsive spending, and unplanned emergencies. The psychology of spending—our vulnerability to instant gratification, advertising, and peer pressure—is far stronger than we imagine. Without tools for stewardship, today's paycheque becomes tomorrow's regret.

Compounding this fragility is the speed with which the financial landscape has transformed. A generation ago, money moved through cheques, savings accounts, and the occasional credit card. Today, the terrain is unrecognisable: digital wallets, contactless payments, cryptocurrencies, buy-now-pay-later schemes. Transactions are frictionless, designed to be invisible, while risks are obscured by novelty. The very vocabulary of finance—blockchains, decentralised ledgers, digital tokens—was alien to policymakers a decade ago, yet it now shapes markets that determine ordinary people's fortunes. To ignore these shifts is to leave young adults navigating a storm without compass or chart.

And yet, the task is not insurmountable. Financial clarity can be built on a few essential habits: budgeting with discipline rather than improvisation, understanding the slow but inexorable power of compounding, recognising debt as both a tool and a trap, distinguishing between assets that grow and liabilities that erode. These are not advanced theories reserved for specialists; they are survival tools every citizen requires. A society that neglects to teach them is not simply careless—it is complicit in perpetuating inequality, leaving competence to the accidents of privilege.

This chapter argues that financial literacy should not be framed as a luxury skill, the preserve of aspiring entrepreneurs or high earners, but as baseline knowledge for survival and dignity. It will explore the cost of financial illiteracy, not in abstract terms but in the lived realities of debt and vulnerability. It will probe the dangerous divide between earning and managing, and why discipline, not income alone, determines stability. It will trace the digital money shift and show why unfamiliarity with these new systems leaves individuals dangerously exposed. And it will introduce a toolkit for clarity—simple, durable practices that allow students to future-proof themselves in an unpredictable economy.

The stakes could not be higher. To be financially illiterate today is to risk more than embarrassment; it is to risk lifelong dependency, stress, and diminished freedom. Money cannot guarantee happiness, but mismanaging it guarantees constraints. If schools will not teach these lessons, then where will the next generation learn them—through predatory contracts, mounting interest, or the quiet erosion of opportunity? The answers are neither comfortable nor simple, but they are urgent. For without a map, every step in the financial world is a gamble—and the house, as ever, is rigged to win.

The Cost of Financial Illiteracy

In the spring of 2017, a survey revealed that nearly two-thirds of Americans could not correctly answer three basic questions on interest rates, inflation, and risk diversification. These were not trick questions—they asked whether borrowing £1,000 at 5% interest would cost more than £1,050 after a year, or whether inflation erodes purchasing power. Yet the majority faltered. The irony was brutal: many of these same individuals were already carrying mortgages, student loans, and credit cards. They were managing thousands of pounds or dollars in transactions without grasping the rules of the game. Imagine stepping into a casino, betting the family's savings, and not knowing how the cards are dealt. That, in essence, is the cost of financial illiteracy.

The stakes are far from theoretical. Debt traps ensnare millions each year: the payday loan with a deceptively small fee that compounds into ruinous interest, the "buy now, pay later" offer that silently multiplies across multiple accounts, the mortgage structured on terms opaque even to educated professionals. Predatory lending thrives precisely because people do not fully understand what they are signing. The documents are dense, the clauses designed to conceal risk, and the customer is too embarrassed—or too rushed—to admit confusion. Schools have produced graduates capable of analysing Shakespearean verse but not a credit contract. The mismatch is costly not only in money but in dignity.

Consider the case of student debt. In the United States, over forty million borrowers owe a collective sum exceeding £1 trillion. Many entered their loans without understanding compound interest, deferment penalties, or the long-term consequences of missed payments. Some chose degrees with modest economic return, financing them with debt that will shadow them for decades. Their lack of financial knowledge did not stem from laziness but from omission. Few had ever been taught the basics of debt management before signing binding contracts at eighteen. The same pattern is replicated elsewhere: in Britain, Australia, and parts of Europe, young adults shoulder loans with little training in how to forecast repayment against projected income.

Financial illiteracy also magnifies inequality. Those from wealthy families often learn informally—through dinner table conversations about mortgages, investments, or tax planning. Their peers without such exposure rely on trial and error, usually costly. The result is a compounding disadvantage: the financially literate accumulate assets, while the illiterate accumulate penalties. By the time both groups reach middle age, one has built equity and stability, the other has amassed debt and insecurity. Schools, ostensibly the great levellers, have widened the gap by neglecting to teach survival knowledge that could mitigate inequality.

The human cost is not confined to numbers on a balance sheet. Chronic debt correlates strongly with stress, anxiety, and depression. Surveys consistently show that financial worries are the leading source of stress for adults, outranking work or health. When every bill induces panic, when every unexpected expense threatens collapse, life shrinks. Relationships fracture, health declines, and opportunity evaporates. To describe financial literacy as optional enrichment, as many curricula implicitly do, is to misunderstand its role. It is not enrichment but emancipation—the knowledge that protects autonomy and preserves dignity.

The paradox is sharpened by the fact that young adults today inhabit an economy more complex than any faced by their parents. A generation ago, financial life meant a savings account, a mortgage, perhaps a pension. Today it is a labyrinth of credit scores, digital wallets, online scams, investment platforms, cryptocurrencies, and microloans. Decisions must be made in real time, often with long-term consequences. Yet curricula remain stuck in the past, treating money as though it were peripheral, even vulgar, unworthy of the classroom. This reticence is costly. Students graduate into a world that monetises their ignorance, and they learn lessons in the harshest possible way: through overdraft fees, foreclosure notices, and the relentless arithmetic of compounding debt.

It is tempting to blame individuals for their financial mistakes. Why sign a contract you do not understand? Why take on debt beyond your means? But this criticism ignores the asymmetry of knowledge and power. Financial institutions employ lawyers, economists, and behavioural scientists to design contracts and marketing strategies. The consumer, often a teenager or young adult, has little more than instinct. To expect equal footing is absurd. Education is the one arena that could redress the imbalance by equipping citizens with baseline competence. Its failure to do so leaves individuals exposed and industries emboldened.

The philosophical dimension is worth pausing over. To be financially illiterate is not merely to risk poverty; it is to risk a form of dependency that undermines freedom itself. A citizen who cannot manage debt is easily manipulated, whether by lenders, employers, or even political actors. Autonomy requires the capacity to make informed choices, and informed choices about money demand knowledge. The philosopher Amartya Sen argued that freedom is not only about formal rights but about real capabilities—the ability to act on one's goals. By this measure, financial literacy is foundational to liberty. Without it, rights are hollow, choices illusory.

Some argue that money is best learned through experience—that the sting of an overdraft teaches more than any classroom ever could. Experience does teach, but at a price. The lesson of predatory lending is often bankruptcy. The lesson of missed pension contributions is discovered only at retirement, when it is too late to adjust. The "school of hard knocks" is efficient but cruel, and its cost is borne most heavily by those who could least afford the tuition. Formal education exists precisely to prevent such wasteful, uneven suffering. Its failure in this domain is glaring.

To frame financial literacy as survival knowledge is not hyperbole. The ability to read a balance sheet, understand an interest rate, or distinguish between asset and liability is as vital to modern life as literacy or numeracy. Without it, individuals are not only disadvantaged—they are vulnerable, prey to systems designed to exploit confusion. The tragedy is that this knowledge is not esoteric. It is teachable, transferable, and transformative. Its absence is not inevitable but chosen, a result of educational priorities frozen in outdated assumptions.

The unresolved question lingers. If schools continue to treat financial competence as peripheral, who will teach it? Parents? Many are themselves unprepared. Employers? Too late, and too self-interested. The marketplace? Only at a price. Until education reclaims its responsibility, the cost of financial illiteracy will be paid daily—by individuals trapped in cycles of debt, by societies weighed down with inequality, and by generations left poorer not only in wealth but in freedom.

Earning vs. Managing

A first paycheque has a way of intoxicating. The graduate, fresh from years of studying, finally sees a number arrive in their bank account larger than any they have known. For a fleeting moment, it feels like freedom. Yet within weeks, perhaps days, the money begins to evaporate—spent on rent, subscriptions, gadgets, holidays taken on credit. The paradox quickly reveals itself: earning is not the same as keeping, and income without management is little more than a mirage.

Modern economies excel at training people to generate income. Schools and universities speak endlessly of employability, career ladders, and the acquisition of marketable skills. But they rarely address what happens next: how to translate wages into security, growth, or freedom. The result is a curious asymmetry. Young adults enter the workforce confident in their capacity to earn but uncertain about how to steward their earnings. They mistake the ability to generate money for the ability to master it.

The psychology of spending explains much of this gap. Human beings are not rational calculators but creatures of desire, habit, and social comparison. Behavioural economists have shown repeatedly that we discount the future heavily, preferring immediate gratification to long-term stability. The pull of a night out, a new phone, or the holiday package is stronger than the dim prospect of retirement three decades away. Credit cards, with their painless swipe and deferred consequence, magnify this bias. The money feels less real when it does not leave our hands. In this context, even the disciplined falter. Without deliberate strategies, income slips through our fingers with the ease of water.

The discipline of managing, by contrast, demands a mindset of resistance. It requires an ability to slow down, to look past the dopamine rush of a purchase and ask whether the expense aligns with longer-term goals. It demands routines—budgeting, saving, investing—that are inherently unglamorous. No one applauds you for transferring £200 into an index fund each month. Yet, over years, such habits separate those who enjoy stability from those who perpetually chase the next paycheque. The contrast between the psychology of spending and the discipline of stewardship is not merely financial; it is philosophical. It reflects two different orientations to life: one reactive, the other intentional.

Examples abound. Professional athletes, whose salaries dwarf those of ordinary citizens, often face bankruptcy within years of retirement. Studies in the United States suggest that nearly 60% of former NBA players are broke within five years of leaving the league. Their problem was never earning; it was managing. Conversely, countless stories exist of immigrants arriving with little, carefully saving, investing modestly but consistently, and building fortunes over time. Their advantage was not extraordinary income but extraordinary discipline. These cases dramatise the same principle: money magnifies habits. If the habit is consumption, income only accelerates depletion. If the habit is stewardship, even modest earnings can compound into wealth.

The cultural context compounds the difficulty. Consumer economies are designed to encourage spending, not saving. Advertising equates consumption with identity. Social media normalises lifestyles financed by debt. The graduate comparing themselves to peers online sees not bank balances but curated images of holidays, homes, and restaurants. To resist this pressure requires more than knowledge—it requires resilience against status anxiety. Financial stewardship is as much an emotional art as it is a mathematical one.

Philosophers from Aristotle to Weber have noted the moral dimensions of money. For Aristotle, the virtue of temperance extended to financial life: an ability to balance desire with prudence. For Weber, the Protestant ethic emphasised discipline, frugality, and delayed gratification as engines of prosperity. Today, stripped of moral or spiritual framing, money management is too often treated as a private inconvenience rather than a civic skill. Yet the consequences of mismanagement ripple beyond the individual. A population living paycheque to paycheque is more vulnerable to political demagoguery, more susceptible to predatory lending, more anxious and less free. In this sense, financial stewardship underpins not only personal wellbeing but the health of democracy itself.

The education system's failure to bridge the gap between earning and managing is striking. We teach students how to maximise income—through degrees, training, credentials—while leaving them to improvise their way through budgeting and investment. The imbalance is akin to training someone to harvest but never to store. It is no wonder that so many find themselves exhausted, always working, yet never secure. Income without management is labour without leverage.

And so the question looms: if earning is celebrated and managing neglected, what future awaits a generation whose income may rise but whose discipline does not? Will higher salaries simply fuel higher consumption, or will individuals learn to resist the current long enough to build lasting stability? The answer is not foregone. It depends on whether we treat financial stewardship as an optional virtue or as essential knowledge—knowledge no less critical than literacy or numeracy. Until then, the paradox will endure: a world full of skilled earners, many of whom remain perpetually broke.

The Digital Money Shift

In the late 20th century, carrying cash was still the dominant ritual of daily commerce. Banknotes and coins changed hands in shops, wages were collected as cheques, and most households balanced their finances by literally balancing a chequebook. Today, the physicality of money is vanishing. For many young adults, wages appear as numbers on a screen, payments are made with the tap of a phone, and saving—or borrowing—happens through interfaces they barely understand. The paradox is stark: money has never been more abstract, yet the consequences of misunderstanding it have never been more concrete.

The shift is not simply from paper to plastic, but from tangible to invisible. Credit cards first eroded the boundary between earning and spending, encouraging consumption on borrowed time. Now digital wallets, contactless payments, and "buy now, pay later" schemes complete the disappearance. A coffee bought on Monday may not register until weeks later when a bloated statement arrives, stripped of the context that once came with handing over cash. Money is no longer experienced as a finite resource but as an infinite stream of transactions, reversible at the swipe of a screen—until, of course, the bill falls due.

Cryptocurrencies add yet another layer of abstraction. For the first time, decentralised systems allow individuals to hold assets outside traditional banks, denominated not in pounds or dollars but in tokens whose value can fluctuate wildly in a single day. Advocates herald this as a democratic revolution, a way to escape the grip of central banks and governments. Yet for the inexperienced, cryptocurrencies are often less revolution than roulette. A generation of young investors has learned this the hard way: fortunes rising overnight, only to collapse in spectacular crashes. Without an understanding of volatility, risk, and the psychology of speculation, digital assets can feel like empowerment even as they hollow out security.

The rapid proliferation of digital financial tools has outpaced the capacity of education systems to prepare users. Schools remain silent on even the basics of interest rates and budgeting, let alone the intricacies of blockchain, fintech platforms, or algorithmic lending. Young adults, therefore, enter a financial landscape of unprecedented complexity armed with knowledge designed for another century. They are asked to navigate systems that did not exist when their teachers were students themselves. The result is predictable: vulnerability to scams, susceptibility to manipulation, and a deep uncertainty about how to distinguish genuine opportunity from digital illusion.

Behavioural science helps explain why the digital shift has proved so treacherous. Humans are evolved to track tangible resources—grain in a silo, coins in a purse. We are far less adept at perceiving abstract flows. Psychologists have shown that people spend more when using cards than cash, because the "pain of paying" is dulled. Digital wallets amplify this effect. The tap of a phone feels frictionless, disembodied from effort. Money loses its weight, and with it, the cues that once encouraged restraint. By design, the digital shift seduces us into treating spending as entertainment rather than decision.

Yet to focus only on the dangers would be misleading. The digital transformation of money carries extraordinary potential. It allows unbanked populations to access credit through mobile phones, empowers individuals to transfer funds globally in seconds, and opens new possibilities for investment and innovation. For those who understand its mechanics, the shift can indeed be liberating. The challenge is that liberation without literacy quickly becomes entrapment. Access to complex tools without the skills to wield them is like placing advanced machinery in the hands of untrained operators—fascinating at first, disastrous in the long run.

The philosophical dimension is profound. When money becomes invisible, trust replaces tangibility. A banknote once embodied value in its physicality. Today, digital balances exist only as records in databases, subject to systems of encryption, regulation, and code. To live in this world is to live in faith—faith in institutions, in algorithms, in the resilience of networks. When these collapse, whether through cyberattacks, market crashes, or institutional failures, the fragility of digital trust becomes visible. For young adults whose education has neglected both the technical and ethical dimensions of finance, this fragility can feel bewildering.

Case studies illustrate the duality. In Kenya, the rise of M-Pesa—a mobile payment platform—has lifted millions out of poverty by enabling secure transfers without traditional banks. Meanwhile, in developed economies, digital platforms have facilitated predatory lending schemes, offering instant credit to consumers already stretched thin. One digital revolution empowers; another exploits. The difference lies in literacy and regulation, in the ability of users to understand terms and anticipate risks. Without these, the same technologies that promise emancipation can accelerate dependency.

The generational stakes are clear. Today's young adults are not only inheriting a digital economy but shaping it. Their financial choices, from whether to save in cryptocurrencies to how they use credit, will ripple across societies. If they are unprepared, the ripple becomes a shockwave: cycles of debt, vulnerability to scams, and widespread disillusionment. If they are prepared, the digital shift could mark the beginning of unprecedented financial inclusion and innovation. The hinge point is not technology itself, but education—the capacity to frame money as a system of choices, risks, and responsibilities rather than a blur of transactions.

Which raises the pressing question: how can societies equip their citizens for a world where money no longer clinks, weighs, or visibly diminishes as it is spent? What forms of literacy are needed when value is stored in algorithms and distributed across invisible networks? And how long can we afford to ignore these questions before the gap between financial reality and financial education grows too wide to close? The digital shift is already here. Whether it becomes a source of empowerment or entrapment will depend less on the technologies themselves than on the wisdom with which they are understood.

A Toolkit for Financial Clarity

In 2019, a young couple in their late twenties walked into a bankruptcy court in London. Both were employed, both earning above the national average. Their problem was not income but clarity. Credit cards, car loans, and a string of subscription payments had created a financial fog they could not pierce. Month after month, money left their accounts faster than it entered, and yet neither could explain exactly where it had gone. They had not gambled, nor lived extravagantly. They had simply lived without structure—no budget, no plan, no understanding of compounding interest beyond its role as an occasional shock on a bank statement. Their story is far from unusual. The absence of simple financial habits does not just erode wealth; it dismantles stability.

The paradox is that these habits are neither complicated nor inaccessible. They are mundane, almost unglamorous, but their effect over time is transformative. Budgeting, compounding, and debt management are not esoteric arts reserved for accountants and financiers. They are survival skills, foundational tools that can determine whether a life is marked by freedom or by perpetual constraint. To neglect them is akin to walking through a storm without a compass: one may keep moving, but not in the right direction.

Budgeting, the first and most essential habit, is often dismissed as tedious bookkeeping. In reality, it is an act of self-awareness. A budget is not simply a spreadsheet; it is a mirror reflecting values. Where money goes, priorities are revealed—sometimes painfully. Tracking spending exposes the silent leakages: the forgotten subscription, the habitual takeaway, the micro-purchases that aggregate into hundreds. More importantly, budgeting transforms anxiety into agency. To know where every pound is allocated is to reclaim control from the vague dread of uncertainty. Whether through the classic "envelope method," digital apps that categorise transactions automatically, or a simple weekly review, the principle is the same: clarity precedes control.

Compounding, by contrast, operates in a quieter register—imperceptible in the short term but seismic over decades. Albert Einstein allegedly called it the "eighth wonder of the world," not because the mathematics are complex but because human psychology consistently underestimates its power. A student who begins investing £100 a month at age twenty-two may, by retirement, accumulate a sum that dwarfs the contributions themselves. The same student, waiting until their thirties to begin, must contribute far more to reach the same outcome. The difference is not income but time—time leveraged through the silent machinery of compounding. To grasp this is to reframe saving not as deprivation but as participation in one of the most reliable engines of growth available to ordinary people.

Debt management completes the toolkit, not as an act of asceticism but as a shield against vulnerability. Debt in itself is not inherently destructive. A mortgage can be a lever for building equity, a student loan an investment in human capital. The danger lies in unmanaged or misunderstood debt. High-interest credit cards, payday loans, and overdraft fees transform short-term convenience into long-term imprisonment. Here again, clarity is the decisive factor. To map debts by interest rate, to prioritise repayment of the most punitive, and to understand the real cost of minimum payments is to move from passivity to strategy. The difference between managing debt and being managed by it is often the difference between stability and collapse.

What unites these habits is not their technical detail but their philosophical significance. Each is an exercise in resisting the immediacy of desire in favour of long-term clarity. Budgeting requires facing reality rather than indulging denial. Compounding requires faith in the future and patience in the present. Debt management requires humility—to recognise limits and act within them. These are not merely financial skills but forms of character. They cultivate discipline, foresight, and resilience—the very traits that underpin flourishing beyond money itself.

Critics might argue that such tools are obvious, that adults inevitably learn them through necessity. Yet evidence suggests otherwise. Surveys in both the United States and Europe reveal that a significant proportion of adults cannot cover an unexpected £400 expense without borrowing. Millions live in cycles of overdraft not from extravagance but from the absence of structure. The cost of ignorance is borne not only by individuals but by societies, in the form of financial crises fuelled by reckless lending and widespread insolvency. To teach financial clarity is therefore not only an act of personal empowerment but a civic responsibility.

The irony is that the very simplicity of these tools often leads to their neglect. They lack the glamour of cryptocurrencies or the drama of stock-market speculation. Yet mastery of the basics is what enables competence in the complex. A graduate who cannot budget should not be lured into day-trading apps. A household without an emergency fund should not dabble in volatile assets. Without a foundation, the edifice collapses. The toolkit is not optional enrichment but prerequisite armour.

Still, the challenge remains: how do we normalise these practices in cultures addicted to immediacy, where financial products are engineered to obscure rather than illuminate? How can schools, workplaces, and families instil habits of clarity when the marketplace profits from confusion? The answer is not yet settled. What is certain is that financial fog leaves individuals vulnerable, while financial clarity equips them to navigate uncertainty with resilience.

The young couple in London might have avoided bankruptcy had they learned to budget, understood compounding, or prioritised debt strategically. Instead, they learned too late, through the unforgiving teacher of experience. The question that lingers is whether we will continue to leave such lessons to chance, or whether we will treat financial clarity as essential knowledge, taught deliberately and early, before mistakes calcify into chains.

Chapter 3
The Unspoken Language of Emotion

On a bright spring morning, a seventeen-year-old pupil sat before his mathematics exam, staring at the paper with a blankness that belied his hours of preparation. He knew the formulas, he had rehearsed the steps, yet his hands shook and his mind seemed to dissolve. Later, his teachers described him as unmotivated, careless, perhaps even lazy. What no one saw was that he was paralysed by anxiety—a physiological storm misinterpreted as indifference. He did not lack ability; he lacked a vocabulary for what was happening inside him. In the silence between mind and body, he failed not because he was incapable but because he was illiterate in the language of emotion.

This is the paradox at the heart of modern education. Schools pride themselves on cultivating intelligence, yet they consistently neglect the form of intelligence most central to human flourishing: the ability to understand, regulate, and communicate emotions. Emotional literacy is not a sentimental luxury, nor a vague "soft skill" tacked on to real learning. It is a fundamental capacity without which relationships fracture, leadership falters, and decision-making veers into distortion. To be blind to one's emotions is to be blind to half of one's life.

The neglect is striking because its consequences are everywhere. Organisations spend billions each year repairing the damage wrought by poor emotional skills—miscommunication, conflict, burnout. Public health systems strain under the weight of stress-related illnesses that might have been mitigated by earlier training in regulation. Individuals themselves wrestle with confusion, mistaking their own signals for flaws: exhaustion reframed as laziness, sadness mislabelled as weakness, anger suppressed until it erupts. A generation schooled in equations and essays emerges into adulthood with no map for navigating its inner terrain.

For centuries, Western thought has perpetuated the myth of rational decision-making: the idea that the mind is a detached instrument, capable of calculating choices free from feeling. Yet modern neuroscience tells a different story. Emotions are not distractions from reason; they are its foundation. Antonio Damasio's research on patients with brain damage to emotional centres showed that when feelings were stripped away, decision-making collapsed. These patients could reason logically, but when faced with real choices—what to eat, what to wear—they were paralysed. To ignore emotion is not to become more rational, but less.

This chapter asks us to consider what education might look like if it recognised emotions as information. Anxiety, for instance, is often pathologised, yet at manageable levels it signals the presence of risk and the need for preparation. Shame, painful though it is, can point to a misalignment between action and value. Even anger, so often feared, carries data about boundaries violated or needs unmet. To suppress these signals is to silence a source of knowledge. The challenge is not to banish emotion but to interpret and regulate it—to turn noise into insight.

Regulation, however, is not suppression. Too often, young people are encouraged to "keep calm" or "push through," advice that confuses repression with resilience. Evidence from psychology suggests the opposite: that naming emotions reduces their intensity, that reflective practices like journaling or mindfulness build clarity, and that constructive expression—through dialogue, art, or physical activity—channels rather than erases energy. Emotional literacy, in this sense, is both diagnostic and prescriptive: it identifies what one feels and offers a repertoire of strategies for responding.

The stakes are as practical as they are philosophical. Leaders who cannot read emotions misinterpret the mood of their teams. Partners who cannot articulate feelings miscommunicate in ways that corrode intimacy. Citizens who cannot regulate anger are more easily manipulated by populist rhetoric. To cultivate emotional literacy, therefore, is not only to enhance individual wellbeing but to safeguard collective life. It is to expand the scope of intelligence to match the complexity of human existence.

And so the pressing question remains: why, if emotions are so central, do we still treat them as peripheral to education? Why does the curriculum measure algebra but not anxiety, essays but not empathy? The answers lie in history, culture, and institutional inertia. Yet the cost of this omission is written daily in workplaces, relationships, and societies strained by misunderstanding. If the 21st century is to be navigated with wisdom, it will demand more than cognitive skill. It will demand fluency in the unspoken language that shapes every decision, every connection, every life. Are we prepared to teach it—or will we continue to leave students to learn it through the slow, costly trial of error?

Why Emotional Literacy Matters

In 1968, a young boy named Walter Mischel conducted a famous experiment at Stanford University, later known as the "marshmallow test." Children were offered a choice: eat one marshmallow immediately, or wait fifteen minutes and receive two. Decades later, researchers tracked the participants into adulthood. The startling result was not that willpower alone predicted their outcomes, but that those who could recognise, regulate, and redirect their emotional impulses tended to perform better across multiple domains—academics, careers, relationships. The lesson was not about sweets; it was about literacy in emotions, the ability to notice desire, manage frustration, and tolerate discomfort. Yet, more than half a century on, schools remain curiously silent on the subject, as if self-control, empathy, or resilience were innate traits rather than teachable skills.

This silence is costly. Emotional literacy—the capacity to understand one's own feelings and those of others, and to act on that understanding—shapes outcomes far more profoundly than many traditional measures of intelligence. It is present in the teacher who can de-escalate conflict by naming a child's frustration, in the doctor who senses the unspoken fear behind a patient's questions, in the leader who inspires loyalty not by command but by emotional resonance. Strip away these skills, and technical expertise alone becomes brittle. A surgeon who lacks empathy may be clinically competent yet traumatises patients; an engineer who cannot manage stress may design brilliantly but burn out. Emotional literacy undergirds not only relationships but performance itself.

The neglect of this form of intelligence reveals a deeper cultural bias. For centuries, Western education has privileged cognition over emotion, treating feelings as distractions to be disciplined rather than sources of insight. The rational mind was revered as the seat of progress, while the emotional life was relegated to private spheres, unworthy of serious study. Yet modern neuroscience dismantles this dichotomy. Antonio Damasio's research demonstrates that emotions are not adversaries of reason but its necessary partners. When brain damage severs emotional processing, decision-making collapses. Emotions, in other words, are not noise in the system—they are the system's guidance signals.

Examples from contemporary life underscore the point. Consider workplace leadership. Studies consistently show that emotional intelligence predicts managerial effectiveness better than raw cognitive ability. The capacity to listen, empathise, and respond to the emotional climate of a team fosters trust, motivation, and creativity. By contrast, leaders who dismiss or suppress emotions often create cultures of fear, where innovation withers and talent flees. Or consider diplomacy: negotiations between nations may hinge less on the technicalities of treaties than on the ability of leaders to read subtle cues, manage hostility, and build rapport. Emotional illiteracy at this level can have geopolitical consequences.

The classroom, paradoxically, may be the least forgiving environment for emotional ignorance. A student paralysed by test anxiety is often mislabelled as careless; one who withdraws due to depression is marked as disengaged. Without literacy, educators misinterpret signals, reinforcing shame rather than alleviating it. Worse, the students themselves internalise these misreadings. They leave school believing they are lazy, incapable, or deficient, when in fact they lacked only the tools to interpret their own emotional data. This is not an individual failing but a systemic blind spot.

The case for teaching emotional literacy, then, is both practical and philosophical. Practically, it equips individuals with strategies for resilience: naming emotions, reframing negative experiences, practising empathy, and building supportive relationships. Philosophically, it challenges the very definition of intelligence. What does it mean to be "educated" if one cannot regulate rage, sit with grief, or recognise joy? Can we truly call someone intelligent if they consistently misinterpret their own inner signals, sabotaging themselves and those around them? By broadening the scope of intelligence to include emotional competence, we acknowledge a fuller picture of human capacity.

And yet, resistance persists. Some argue that emotions are too subjective to be taught, that they belong to private upbringing rather than public education. But this argument collapses under scrutiny. We teach literature not because everyone will interpret Shakespeare identically, but because shared frameworks enrich understanding. Emotional literacy is no different. Teaching children to identify emotions, to practise perspective-taking, or to regulate stress does not impose uniformity; it equips them with a grammar for navigating human experience. The alternative is leaving them to guess, to stumble through adulthood with the emotional vocabulary of a child.

What remains unresolved is not whether emotional literacy matters, but whether institutions are willing to prioritise it. In a world marked by polarisation, climate anxiety, and technological upheaval, the capacity to navigate emotions is no longer peripheral. It is central to survival, cohesion, and progress. The question that lingers, unsettlingly, is this: if we continue to neglect emotions in education, what kind of society are we cultivating—one of technically skilled but emotionally impoverished individuals, or one prepared to meet the complexity of life with both intellect and empathy?

The Myth of Rational Decision-Making

In the aftermath of a car accident, a man sits across from his doctor. The damage to his brain is subtle but devastating: the regions that process emotion have been impaired. Strangely, his memory remains intact, his reasoning skills untouched. He can calculate, recite, and analyse with precision. And yet, when asked to decide whether to schedule his next appointment for Tuesday or Wednesday, he falters. He lists the pros and cons endlessly, paralysed by the choice. Without emotion, he cannot decide. This is not fiction but fact, drawn from the pioneering research of neurologist Antonio Damasio, who demonstrated that feelings are not obstacles to rationality—they are its engine.

For centuries, the Western ideal of the rational human being—the *homo economicus* of economists, the dispassionate thinker of philosophers—has cast emotion as a contaminant, a dangerous intrusion into the clarity of thought. Logic, it was said, requires distance from passion; the heart is the enemy of the mind. Yet modern psychology and neuroscience paint a very different picture: emotions are not the antithesis of reason, but its indispensable partner. Every choice we make, from the trivial to the life-altering, is saturated with feeling. To ignore this truth is not to transcend bias but to become its unwitting captive.

Consider the marketplace. Traditional economic theory assumes consumers weigh options with mathematical precision, calculating costs and benefits before arriving at rational choices. In reality, purchases are driven as much by fear of missing out, status anxiety, or nostalgia as by price tags. Advertising industries thrive on this truth, deploying images, colours, and stories that bypass logic and tap directly into emotion. A child's toy sells not because of its specifications but because it promises belonging, joy, or parental approval. Markets, in practice, are theatres of emotion masquerading as arenas of reason.

The influence of feeling is no less evident in politics. Voters often justify their choices with policy arguments after the fact, but studies show that the initial pull is emotional: trust in a leader's face, resonance with a narrative, or identification with a group. Political campaigns do not merely present facts; they orchestrate atmospheres. Slogans, chants, and symbols stir collective feeling long before logic takes the stage. To imagine that citizens cast ballots on purely rational grounds is to mistake the surface for the substance.

Education, however, still clings to the myth. Students are encouraged to separate mind from feeling, as if decisions about careers, ethics, or relationships could ever be made in a vacuum. The consequence is paradoxical: by dismissing emotions as distractions, we leave students more vulnerable to their sway. A pupil taught that fear or shame is irrelevant to learning may misinterpret those signals as personal failure, when in fact they are integral to the decision to persist, withdraw, or seek help. Rationality without recognition of emotion is not strength but fragility.

The science of cognitive biases illustrates the point with precision. Confirmation bias, the tendency to favour evidence that supports our beliefs, is driven less by logic than by the discomfort of dissonance. Loss aversion—the tendency to fear losses more than we value gains—emerges from the emotional weight of regret. These are not quirks of thought alone; they are the fingerprints of feeling on judgement. Attempts to correct them through logic alone often fail, because they do not address the underlying emotional dynamics.

Yet to acknowledge the role of emotion is not to surrender to irrationality. It is to harness a fuller picture of human decision-making. Emotions act as heuristics, compressing complex information into intuitive signals. A gut feeling of unease in a negotiation may reflect countless subtle cues: a tone of voice, a shift in posture, a remembered pattern of deceit. Such intuitions are not infallible, but neither are they irrelevant. Properly trained, they become assets—emotional data that complement logical analysis.

Philosophy, too, offers perspective. Aristotle argued that virtue lies not in suppressing emotion but in cultivating it—anger in the right amount, at the right time, towards the right object. The Stoics, often caricatured as cold, in fact counselled not eradication of feeling but mastery over it. The task was not to expel passion but to shape it towards reasoned ends. Modern science echoes this ancient wisdom: the best decisions arise not from the absence of emotion but from its integration with thought.

The practical implications are profound. In classrooms, teaching students to identify and regulate their emotions could enhance—not diminish—their capacity for sound decision-making. In workplaces, leaders who acknowledge the emotional undercurrents of choices can steer teams with greater clarity and resilience. In personal life, recognising the role of feeling can prevent paralysis, as with Damasio's patients, and foster decisions that are both rational and humane.

And yet, a tension remains. If every decision is shaped by emotion, how can we trust our judgement? How do we distinguish between feelings that illuminate and those that mislead? The challenge is not to exile emotion from the process but to cultivate literacy: to name, interrogate, and refine our feelings as part of the decision itself. The myth of pure rationality crumbles under scrutiny, but what replaces it is not chaos. It is a more intricate picture of human intelligence—one in which the heart and mind are not adversaries, but partners. The unresolved question is whether our institutions will adapt, or whether they will continue to produce students fluent in equations but mute in the language that shapes every choice they will ever make.

Recognizing Hidden Signals

In 2017, a secondary school teacher in Manchester described one of her pupils as "lazy." He never completed homework, avoided speaking up in class, and seemed to slump deeper into his chair with every passing week. Months later, it emerged that he had been struggling with severe anxiety: sleepless nights, constant stomach aches, and a paralysing fear of failure. What looked like apathy was, in fact, exhaustion; what appeared as disinterest was self-preservation. His story is not an anomaly. Across classrooms, workplaces, and homes, anxiety, stress, and shame are misread as laziness, incompetence, or lack of discipline. We treat them as personal flaws rather than signals—vital data about the pressures individuals are carrying and the adjustments they might need.

The paradox is that these hidden signals often masquerade as weakness precisely because they remain unrecognised. Anxiety can look like avoidance: the student who never starts the essay, the employee who procrastinates on emails. Stress can look like irritability or distraction: the parent snapping at their child, the colleague who forgets small tasks. Shame can look like withdrawal: the young adult retreating into silence, the high achiever suddenly disengaging. From the outside, the behaviour seems inexplicable. From the inside, it is a strategy for survival. Misinterpretation not only perpetuates stigma but denies the opportunity for growth.

The science of emotion reframes these experiences. Anxiety is not merely an enemy to be eliminated; it is an evolved response to potential threat. In moderation, it sharpens attention, primes the body for action, and signals that something matters. Chronic anxiety, of course, overwhelms these functions, but the underlying signal is meaningful: it tells us where we feel vulnerable, where preparation or support is needed. Stress operates similarly. Short bursts of stress can enhance performance, heightening focus and energy. Only when it becomes relentless does it erode health. Even shame, often dismissed as toxic, has a signalling role. It reveals where one perceives a rupture between action and values, pointing to the need for repair or realignment. To discard these signals wholesale is to discard information vital to self-awareness.

Modern psychology and neuroscience support this reframing. Studies of "emotional granularity"—the ability to identify emotions with precision—show that individuals who can distinguish between feeling "anxious," "overwhelmed," and "uneasy" cope more effectively than those who lump all discomfort into "bad." Labelling emotions accurately engages the brain's prefrontal cortex, creating space between the feeling and the response. In this sense, recognising hidden signals is not indulgence but intelligence. It allows the individual to harness information rather than drown in it.

Real-world examples illustrate the stakes. In the workplace, an employee's missed deadlines may be attributed to laziness. But closer examination might reveal burnout: long hours, unclear expectations, or lack of autonomy. Addressing the behaviour with punishment deepens the problem; addressing the signal with support can transform it. In education, students often branded as "unmotivated" are those most crippled by fear of failure. Research on self-determination theory shows that when environments foster autonomy, competence, and relatedness, motivation resurfaces. Recognising signals, then, is not an act of indulgence but a pathway to effectiveness.

Philosophically, the misinterpretation of these signals reveals a cultural blind spot. Many societies still prize stoicism, equating silence with strength and expression with weakness. The narrative is seductive: grit through discomfort, bury emotion, keep going. Yet the cost of this suppression is evident in the epidemics of anxiety and burnout that plague both students and professionals. To deny signals is to drive blind, mistaking speed for progress. True resilience is not the absence of discomfort but the ability to interpret it wisely.

It is also a matter of justice. Misreading hidden signals disproportionately affects the vulnerable. Children from disadvantaged backgrounds may be more likely to internalise shame and anxiety due to systemic pressures, only to be labelled as "problem students." Employees in precarious work environments may hide stress until collapse, fearing stigma or job loss. By recognising signals as data rather than defects, we move towards environments that are not only more humane but more equitable.

Of course, recognition alone is not enough. To notice anxiety is not to cure it; to name shame is not to dissolve it. But recognition is the essential first step. Without it, strategies of regulation—breathing, reframing, seeking support—cannot even begin. The mislabelling of emotional signals as laziness short-circuits growth, replacing curiosity with judgement. With recognition, however, discomfort becomes a compass: it points not just to what is wrong, but to what matters most.

The challenge is cultural as much as individual. How do we train ourselves, our educators, and our leaders to ask not only "What is wrong with this person?" but "What might this behaviour be signalling?" How do we build institutions that see anxiety, stress, and shame not as failings to punish but as data to interpret? The answers are still unfolding. What is clear is that failing to recognise these signals comes at a cost: wasted potential, broken trust, and lives misread. The unresolved question is whether we will continue to mistake hidden signals for flaws—or whether we will learn, finally, to listen to what they are trying to tell us.

From Suppression to Regulation

In the early twentieth century, schoolchildren were often taught to keep "a stiff upper lip." Displays of sadness or anger were swiftly corrected; stoicism was considered virtue, vulnerability a flaw. Fast forward a century, and the echoes remain. Many students still learn, explicitly or implicitly, that the best response to difficult emotions is to push them down, contain them, and move on. The paradox is that suppression rarely eliminates the feeling—it intensifies it. What is hidden festers. The child who buries frustration may erupt in aggression later; the student who smothers anxiety may find it leaking into physical symptoms, sleepless nights, or unexplained fatigue. Suppression is not strength but a brittle façade.

The alternative is regulation: not the eradication of emotion, but its intelligent management. Regulation acknowledges that emotions are inevitable, even necessary, but insists they can be shaped and channelled in ways that serve rather than sabotage. This distinction matters. A pupil who tries to suppress stage fright before a presentation may find their voice trembling uncontrollably. One who instead uses regulation techniques—deep breathing, reframing nerves as excitement, visualising success—can convert the same surge of adrenaline into energy and focus. Regulation does not deny emotion; it translates it into usable force.

Evidence supports this shift. Research from James Gross at Stanford University shows that suppression, while it may reduce outward expression, often amplifies physiological stress and impairs memory. Regulation strategies such as cognitive reappraisal—rethinking the meaning of a situation—by contrast, reduce distress and improve performance. Students who reinterpret a poor grade not as proof of incompetence but as feedback for growth recover more quickly and persist longer. Similarly, mindfulness practices, now extensively studied, train individuals to observe emotions without immediate reaction, creating space between impulse and response. These are not abstract philosophies but practical tools, teachable and learnable.

Real-world examples illuminate the difference. In professional sport, athletes are drilled not only in physical skill but in emotional regulation. The tennis player who channels frustration into focus may seize momentum; the one who smashes a racket often spirals into defeat. In business, leaders who regulate stress project calm that steadies teams in crisis. Those who suppress anxiety may appear composed, but their inauthenticity leaks out, eroding trust.

Regulation, unlike suppression, sustains both performance and relationships.

The cultural reluctance to embrace regulation reflects deeper discomfort with emotions themselves. We live in societies that reward productivity and control, often at the expense of reflection and nuance. Yet regulation is not indulgence. It is efficiency of a higher order: the capacity to respond in ways aligned with values and goals. A student who recognises the onset of shame and speaks to a mentor rather than retreating into silence is not being "soft." They are deploying strategy. They are conserving energy for growth rather than wasting it in battle with themselves.

Philosophically, regulation raises profound questions about freedom. If emotions are inevitable, then suppression represents a denial of reality. Regulation, however, offers a path to agency: by engaging with emotions, we gain choice in how to act. The Stoics, so often misunderstood, captured this distinction. They did not advocate emotional numbness but emphasised the discipline of interpretation—deciding how to perceive events, and thus how to feel and act. Regulation is this philosophy in practice, a modern articulation of an ancient insight.

The question, then, is not whether students feel emotions—they always will—but whether they are given the tools to navigate them. Imagine classrooms where emotional literacy is treated as seriously as mathematics: where pupils learn to identify stress signals, practise techniques of reappraisal, and build repertoires of coping strategies. Such education would not only reduce anxiety and improve concentration, but also prepare students for adult life, where pressures multiply and emotional resilience becomes a determinant of health, relationships, and leadership.

And yet, resistance lingers. Some fear that teaching regulation will soften students, leaving them ill-prepared for hardship. But the opposite is true. Suppression produces fragility: the inability to cope when emotions inevitably surge. Regulation produces flexibility: the capacity to bend without breaking. The open question is whether our institutions are willing to abandon outdated ideals of stoicism in favour of this more sophisticated vision. Until they do, we will continue to graduate students trained to solve equations and memorise dates, but untrained in the more urgent task—what to do when their heart races, their stomach knots, or their voice trembles at the threshold of life's challenges.

Chapter 4
Thinking in an Age of Noise

On the morning of 6 January 2021, a crowd stormed the United States Capitol. Many of those who forced their way into the chambers of government believed, with unwavering conviction, that they were defending democracy. Their certainty was not born of careful evidence but of a steady diet of misinformation, amplified and reinforced by algorithms that rewarded outrage over accuracy. It was a spectacle of conviction without clarity, of passion untethered from truth. In the chaos of that day lay a lesson as urgent as it was unsettling: trust in information, once fractured, is hard to restore.

We live in an age where every headline, video, and post clamours for our attention. The sheer volume of information available at any given moment would dwarf the lifetime reading capacity of our ancestors. Yet more information does not mean more clarity. Instead, it has created a landscape where truth competes on equal terms with falsehood, where algorithms filter reality to our biases, and where noise masquerades as knowledge. In such a world, the capacity to think critically is not optional enrichment; it is survival. To navigate without it is to become manipulable—drifting with whichever current of influence happens to pull most strongly.

The problem is not only external but internal. Our brains, far from being objective processors of information, come equipped with biases that shape what we notice, what we ignore, and what we believe. Confirmation bias drives us to seek evidence that supports our preconceptions; the availability heuristic tricks us into overestimating the importance of vivid or recent events; anchoring tethers us to the first figure we hear, even when it is irrelevant. These cognitive shortcuts, once adaptive in environments of scarcity and simplicity, now leave us vulnerable in an environment of abundance and complexity. The flood of information meets the flaws of human cognition, and the result is distortion.

History offers perspective. In the early days of print, the explosion of pamphlets spread not only new ideas but also wild rumours and dangerous fabrications. The invention of the printing press did not automatically usher in enlightenment; it required the parallel development of norms, institutions, and skills to distinguish fact from fiction. The digital revolution has triggered a similar upheaval, but this time on a scale and speed that dwarf anything seen before. We are once again in the infancy of a new information age, and the stakes are higher: misinformation does not merely mislead, it shapes elections, fuels conflict, and corrodes trust in science, medicine, and democracy itself.

Critical thinking, then, must be reframed. It is not merely an academic skill deployed in the margins of essays, nor a distant cousin of logic puzzles to be solved for marks. It is a civic virtue, a personal shield, and a compass. To interrogate sources, to test credibility, to spot logical fallacies—these are acts of resistance against manipulation. They allow individuals to withstand persuasion not by closing themselves off in cynicism, but by standing firm in discernment. The aim is not to doubt everything but to question wisely, to cultivate resilience in the face of persuasion without surrendering to paranoia.

Consider a student scrolling through social media. An emotionally charged post claims that a new vaccine is dangerous, citing a shadowy "study." Without the ability to interrogate sources—Who conducted the study? Is it peer-reviewed? What do experts in the field say?—the student is likely to accept or reject the claim based on emotional resonance alone. Multiply this by millions, and the fragility of public understanding becomes clear. The ability to pause, to question, to dig deeper is not only the mark of an educated person; it is the bedrock of a functioning society.

Yet the challenge extends beyond misinformation to persuasion itself. Human beings are inherently social, and persuasion is the currency of our interactions. Advertisers, political campaigns, influencers—all seek to shape behaviour. Building a mind that can withstand persuasion does not mean refusing to be influenced; it means cultivating awareness of how influence works and choosing consciously which appeals to accept. It means recognising when emotion is being weaponised, when repetition is being used to simulate truth, when group identity is being exploited to silence dissent. It is the difference between being carried along unconsciously and steering deliberately.

The task ahead is both urgent and daunting. How do we train minds to navigate this cacophony without succumbing to despair? How do we teach scepticism without breeding cynicism, resilience without hardening into distrust? The answers will require more than pedagogy; they will demand a cultural shift in how we value and practise thinking itself. The danger of failing to adapt is clear: citizens adrift in noise, unable to tell signal from distortion, paralysed or deceived at the very moments when judgement is most needed. The opportunity, however, is equally clear: to cultivate a generation for whom discernment is instinct, for whom critical thinking is not a luxury but a way of seeing. The question is whether we will rise to the challenge—or allow the noise to think for us.

The Collapse of Trust in Information

In the spring of 2020, a video claiming that a shadowy cabal had engineered the coronavirus pandemic spread across the internet at lightning speed. It was professionally shot, laced with jargon, and shared millions of times before major platforms scrambled to remove it. For many who watched, the slick presentation was indistinguishable from legitimate science. Neighbours argued, families fractured, and public health campaigns faltered—all because one piece of misinformation found fertile ground in a moment of fear. It was a stark reminder that in the digital age, the line between knowledge and deception is not guarded by experts at the gate but blurred by the algorithms that shape our feeds.

The paradox of our time is that we have never had more access to information, yet trust in information has rarely been lower. The internet promised a democratisation of knowledge, and in some respects it delivered: encyclopaedias replaced by Wikipedia, libraries accessible from a smartphone. But the same channels that distribute credible research also distribute conspiracy theories, fabricated statistics, and deepfake videos. The flood is indiscriminate. For the average student or citizen, it is increasingly difficult to tell the difference between fact and fabrication. The result is a crisis not just of truth but of trust.

What makes this collapse so dangerous is that it exploits our natural cognitive shortcuts. Human beings are not designed to verify every piece of information they encounter; we evolved in small groups where knowledge travelled by reputation and proximity. Trusting the word of a neighbour or elder was usually enough. In today's environment, those instincts betray us. We are more likely to believe what confirms our worldview, what is repeated often, or what comes wrapped in authority signals—slick graphics, confident tone, apparent expertise. The manipulability of human cognition meets the mechanics of the attention economy, and the outcome is predictable: misinformation thrives.

Consider how algorithms amplify the problem. Social media platforms are engineered to reward engagement, not accuracy. Content that provokes outrage spreads faster than content that informs. A nuanced explanation of vaccine safety will languish, while a sensational claim about hidden dangers will go viral. Students who consume their news primarily through such platforms are, in effect, being trained to privilege emotional impact over evidential weight. To fail to question information in this landscape is to surrender one's judgement to the invisible hand of code optimised for profit.

The consequences are not abstract. When large swathes of the population distrust election results despite evidence, democratic institutions wobble. When conspiracy theories about climate change outcompete scientific consensus, policies stall while the planet warms. When health misinformation circulates faster than medical advice, lives are lost unnecessarily. The cost of misplaced trust is measured not only in confusion but in bodies, ballots, and futures.

Philosophically, the collapse of trust in information strikes at something deeper: the fabric of shared reality. Societies function because enough people can agree on a set of facts against which to debate values. Without that baseline, argument itself becomes impossible. If one person insists the earth is flat while another insists it is round, dialogue collapses. When groups retreat into isolated echo chambers, each with its own "truth," public discourse fragments into parallel monologues. The danger is not merely that people are wrong, but that they no longer believe in the possibility of right and wrong at all.

And yet, scepticism alone is not sufficient. To respond by doubting everything is to replace naivety with paralysis. What is required is critical discernment: the cultivated skill of interrogating information without descending into cynicism. Students must learn to ask not only "Is this true?" but "Who produced this? For what purpose? With what evidence?" They must learn to recognise logical fallacies, to trace claims to their sources, to distinguish between expertise and posturing. These are not arcane academic exercises but practical survival skills in a world where every scroll, click, or share is a test of discernment.

The challenge is monumental, but it is also an opportunity. The collapse of trust in information exposes the inadequacy of old educational models that treat knowledge as static and authority as unquestionable. It demands a new pedagogy—one that prepares students not simply to absorb facts but to interrogate them, to weigh evidence, and to live with ambiguity. The open question is whether schools, universities, and societies at large are willing to embrace this challenge before the costs become irreparable.

If trust has collapsed, it can be rebuilt—but only with vigilance, humility, and a recognition that in the age of noise, thinking is not passive reception but active defence. The flood will not recede. The task before us is to learn how to stand within it without being swept away.

Cognitive Biases at Work

On 22 October 1962, President John F. Kennedy and his advisors debated how to respond to Soviet missiles discovered in Cuba. The stakes were existential; miscalculation could trigger nuclear war. Yet even in that room of seasoned statesmen, the gravitational pull of cognitive bias was evident. Hawks overestimated the likelihood of military success, doves clung to selective evidence of Soviet restraint, and both sides viewed their own assumptions as objective truth. Kennedy's eventual choice of a naval blockade—somewhere between appeasement and attack—was less the product of perfect rationality than of navigating human bias under extraordinary pressure. The Cuban Missile Crisis is remembered as a triumph of cool-headed leadership, but beneath the legend lies a more sobering truth: even the most powerful minds are not free of psychological distortion.

The illusion of human rationality has long been one of our most comforting myths. We like to believe that decisions—whether about politics, finances, or daily life—stem from careful reasoning, that we weigh evidence impartially before choosing. Behavioural science dismantles this assumption. Decades of research by figures such as Daniel Kahneman and Amos Tversky have shown that our reasoning is not a neutral calculator but a storytelling machine. It privileges coherence over accuracy, speed over rigour, and confidence over doubt. Cognitive biases are not rare glitches in an otherwise rational system; they are the default settings of the human mind.

Take confirmation bias, perhaps the most pervasive of all. Faced with ambiguous evidence, we naturally privilege what supports our pre-existing beliefs and discount what challenges them. A student researching climate change might uncritically accept an article that aligns with their political views while dismissing equally credible but contradictory data. In a world saturated with selective information, confirmation bias is not simply a private quirk; it is a public hazard. It hardens ideological divides, fuels conspiracy theories, and ensures that debates often generate more heat than light.

The availability heuristic illustrates a different but equally insidious distortion. This bias leads us to overestimate the likelihood of events that are vivid or recent. After a high-profile plane crash, many travellers irrationally fear flying, even though statistically their risk of accident has barely changed. Media outlets, attuned to our susceptibility, amplify such distortions: crime appears rampant when news cycles dwell on isolated but dramatic incidents. Students, growing up in this environment, may carry an inflated sense of danger or opportunity, shaping life choices not by probabilities but by salience.

Anchoring bias demonstrates how first impressions stubbornly shape our decisions. In experiments, individuals asked to estimate the percentage of African nations in the UN gave markedly different answers depending on whether they had first spun a random number wheel. The arbitrary "anchor" exerted gravitational pull, despite irrelevance. Anchoring affects everything from salary negotiations to online shopping. A student might overpay for rent simply because the landlord's opening price feels like the baseline, even when it has no relation to market value.

Then there is the Dunning–Kruger effect, which captures the tragicomic reality that those who know least often feel most confident. Inexperienced individuals lack not only competence but the self-awareness to recognise their incompetence. Conversely, the more skilled often underestimate their abilities, assuming others find tasks as easy as they do. In classrooms and workplaces alike, this bias distorts evaluations of talent, promotes misplaced confidence, and sometimes elevates the wrong voices.

What makes biases particularly treacherous is that they masquerade as common sense. They operate below the threshold of awareness, shaping our perceptions before reason enters the scene. Kahneman distinguishes between *System 1*—fast, intuitive, emotional—and *System 2*—slow, deliberative, analytical. Biases live in System 1, offering shortcuts that conserve energy but often at the cost of accuracy. To resist them requires not only awareness but active effort: a slowing down of thought, a willingness to entertain disconfirming evidence, a deliberate cultivation of intellectual humility.

Yet the story of bias is not only about error. These shortcuts evolved because they once served us well. In ancestral environments, rapid judgement—deciding whether a rustle in the grass signalled predator or wind—could mean the difference between survival and death. The problem arises when the same shortcuts are applied to complex, modern decisions. A brain designed for immediacy struggles with the abstract, statistical, and probabilistic reasoning demanded by twenty-first-century life. The mismatch is structural: evolutionary legacy collides with modern complexity.

The implications for education are profound. If students are taught to memorise facts but not to interrogate the mental machinery that processes those facts, they will remain vulnerable. Knowledge of bias must itself become part of the curriculum—not as a dry catalogue of psychological curiosities but as a practical toolkit. Recognising confirmation bias in oneself, adjusting for anchoring in negotiations, or countering availability distortions with statistical literacy—these are as essential as algebra or grammar.

The workplace, too, offers daily laboratories of bias. Hiring managers overvalue candidates who resemble themselves (similarity bias). Investors chase rising stocks while ignoring fundamentals (herd behaviour). Doctors misdiagnose rare conditions because the common explanation springs more easily to mind (representativeness heuristic). Biases, in other words, are not abstract; they shape salaries, portfolios, diagnoses, and justice. To study them is not to indulge in theory but to grapple with the mechanisms that direct the trajectories of lives.

The deeper philosophical challenge is this: if our thinking is so riddled with distortion, what becomes of free will and responsibility? Are we merely puppets of our biases, condemned to repeat errors? The answer lies in recognising the distinction between inevitability and tendency. Biases nudge, but they do not dictate. With self-awareness, feedback, and structures that promote accountability, individuals and societies can mitigate their influence. The task is not to become perfectly rational—a fantasy—but to become rational enough, to cultivate practices that tilt the balance towards clarity.

Still, the unresolved tension remains. Even as behavioural science maps our biases, those very biases distort how we receive the science. We nod at descriptions of confirmation bias, immediately applying them to others rather than ourselves. We acknowledge anchoring yet remain swayed by the first price we see. Knowledge does not automatically translate into mastery. The gap between insight and application is stubborn.

And so the question lingers, pressing and uncomfortable: if even awareness of bias is not enough to free us, what structures—educational, cultural, technological—are needed to guard our collective judgement? Until we answer it, the hidden puppeteers of bias will continue their quiet work, shaping choices that feel rational but rarely are.

Learning to Interrogate Sources

In October 1938, millions of Americans tuned their radios to what they thought was a breaking news broadcast. Reports of Martians landing in New Jersey, complete with panicked eyewitness accounts and expert commentary, sent listeners into genuine terror. Of course, it was Orson Welles's infamous *War of the Worlds* radio play, not an invasion. The fact that so many believed it reminds us of something sobering: human beings are deeply vulnerable to the packaging of information, not just its content. We trust the trappings of authority—confident voices, apparent expertise, polished presentation—often without interrogating what lies beneath. Eighty years later, with misinformation proliferating on platforms that update by the second rather than the hour, the same susceptibility threatens our collective capacity for sound judgement.

The paradox of the digital age is that we have never had such abundant access to knowledge, nor such abundant access to falsehood. The same device that can stream a peer-reviewed lecture can also push us towards a conspiracy theory through a persuasive headline or an algorithmically curated thread. The distinction between credible knowledge and manipulative content has become perilously blurred. For students navigating this landscape, the failure to question a source is not a minor lapse; it can shape careers, political identities, and even democratic stability.

So how does one interrogate a source in a world where authority is diffuse, attention fleeting, and truth contested? The starting point is deceptively simple: ask *who* is speaking and *why*. When a health influencer on social media insists that vaccines are dangerous, the critical thinker asks about their training, their funding, their incentives. Are they qualified in epidemiology, or are they monetising outrage through clicks and sponsorships? Asking about authorship is not an act of cynicism but of context-setting. It reminds us that information always emerges from a position, and that position is rarely neutral.

But authorship alone is insufficient. Sources must be tested against evidence. Claims require verification, and the habit of triangulation—checking multiple independent outlets or data points—is indispensable. Consider the spread of deepfakes: a video may appear convincing, yet without corroborating evidence, it cannot be trusted. Here, scepticism is not paralysis but prudence: the refusal to grant certainty until claims withstand scrutiny. One of the most valuable lessons students can learn is that truth is rarely established by a single loud voice but by a convergence of consistent, credible signals.

Logical fallacies present another trap. Misinformation often thrives not because it fabricates data but because it packages arguments in ways that appeal emotionally while failing logically. The ad hominem attack, for instance, discredits an opponent by mocking their character rather than their evidence. The straw man reframes an argument in its weakest possible form, then defeats it. The slippery slope warns that a small policy change will inevitably spiral into catastrophe. These fallacies are seductive because they mimic reasoning; they *feel* persuasive while bypassing the rigour of thought. Teaching students to identify such moves—spotting the leap, the misdirection, the rhetorical sleight of hand—is like inoculating them against manipulation.

Nor should we underestimate the subtle power of design. A website with sleek graphics, a video with confident narration, or a report printed in professional typeface can project legitimacy even if the content is baseless. Similarly, virality confers the illusion of credibility: when a million people share a headline, it seems more believable, even though popularity and truth are not synonyms. The philosopher John Stuart Mill argued that truth emerges through the clash of ideas, but in the age of algorithms, ideas do not always clash—they often cluster into echo chambers. The interrogator of sources must therefore look not only at content but at the environment of circulation: is this information being tested across perspectives, or simply amplified within a closed loop of agreement?

The practical skills for source interrogation are not arcane. They include reverse-image searches to check whether a photo has been recycled from another event. They involve learning to parse domains—distinguishing peer-reviewed journals from predatory lookalikes, reputable outlets from pseudo-news sites designed to mimic them. They require the discipline of slowing down, resisting the urge to share before verifying, pausing to ask: *does this align too neatly with what I already believe?* That last question is crucial, because as behavioural science shows, our biases collude with misinformation. We are most likely to trust what flatters our worldview.

Philosophically, the task of interrogating sources is about more than protecting ourselves from deception. It is about cultivating intellectual autonomy. To question information is to assert one's agency, to refuse to be a passive consumer of narratives crafted by others. It is also, paradoxically, an act of humility: recognising that our own first impressions are unreliable, that we need external checks and diverse perspectives to approach truth. In that sense, interrogating sources is both a defensive and a generative act—shielding us from manipulation while opening us to deeper understanding.

Yet a tension remains unresolved. Critical scrutiny can guard against error, but it can also slide into corrosive scepticism. If we question everything, do we risk believing nothing? At what point does the interrogation of sources cease to clarify and instead paralyse? This is the line students must learn to walk: between gullibility and nihilism, between uncritical trust and endless doubt. The tools exist, the practices are teachable, but the balance is delicate. And in a world where the noise of falsehood grows louder each day, the question presses with urgency: how do we build minds that can interrogate without despair, discern without dismissing, and hold on to truth when the very idea of truth is under siege?

Building a Mind That Can Withstand Persuasion

In 1978, more than nine hundred people died in the Guyanese jungle after drinking cyanide-laced punch at the urging of Jim Jones, the leader of the Peoples Temple. The event, remembered as Jonestown, is often invoked as a symbol of blind faith, but at its heart lies a chilling lesson about persuasion. These were not foolish or ignorant people; many were educated, civic-minded, and deeply committed to ideals of equality and justice. What they lacked was not intelligence but the mental armour to withstand manipulative authority. When confronted with charismatic leadership, social pressure, and the gradual erosion of doubt, even strong minds can collapse. The question that haunts us is stark: how does one build an inner compass sturdy enough to resist such coercion, while still remaining open to truth?

The danger is not confined to cults or fringe movements. Every day, individuals are nudged, coaxed, and steered—by advertisers who exploit cognitive shortcuts, by politicians who inflame fear, by technology platforms that optimise for attention rather than accuracy. Persuasion itself is not inherently malicious; indeed, much of civic life depends upon it. The problem arises when persuasion overrides autonomy, when external voices drown out internal discernment. Resilience, in this context, means neither gullibility nor reflexive suspicion, but the cultivation of habits that preserve clarity amid pressure.

To withstand persuasion, one must first recognise its tools. Robert Cialdini's landmark work on influence identified principles such as reciprocity, authority, scarcity, and social proof as levers that can bypass rational scrutiny. Consider scarcity: the "limited-time offer" that compels us to act before we think. Or social proof: the viral trend that gains credibility by sheer popularity. These mechanisms operate beneath awareness, tugging at primal instincts rather than reasoned deliberation. A resilient mind does not deny these impulses but names them, pauses before them, and creates the space in which choice can breathe.

This space—the gap between stimulus and response—is the foundation of resilience. Viktor Frankl, the psychiatrist and Holocaust survivor, famously wrote of this gap as the locus of freedom. To cultivate it requires deliberate training. Practices such as mindfulness, critical self-questioning, and deliberate exposure to opposing viewpoints all extend the interval between persuasion and assent. For students especially, this is transformative: rather than reacting reflexively to authority or peer norms, they can learn to observe their own reactions, interrogate them, and decide with intention.

Yet resilience is not merely defensive. It is also constructive: the capacity to anchor one's thinking in principles that withstand external pressure. Philosophers from the Stoics to Kant have argued that freedom lies not in resisting all influence but in discerning which influences are worthy of assent. The Stoic would counsel detachment from passions that cloud judgement; Kant would urge us to act according to principles we could will as universal. Both traditions converge on the idea that autonomy requires an internal compass—values and heuristics tested against reason, not simply absorbed from environment.

Modern cognitive science reinforces this view. Studies on "cognitive immunology" suggest that exposing individuals to weakened forms of misleading arguments—like a vaccine exposes the body to a weakened pathogen—can build resistance. This process, known as "inoculation theory," demonstrates that resilience is teachable. Students who practice refuting manipulative arguments are less likely to succumb to them later. In a sense, the mind becomes fortified not by insulation but by deliberate encounters with persuasion under conditions of reflection.

Still, resilience cannot mean retreat into cynicism. The cynic, who dismisses all persuasion as manipulation, closes themselves off to truth as effectively as the gullible open themselves to falsehood. The goal is not impenetrability but permeability with discernment. A society of cynics, unable to trust any institution, collapses into fragmentation and paralysis. Thus, resilience must be framed not as blanket resistance but as calibrated receptivity: the art of discerning when to stand firm and when to be moved.

This calibration depends on humility. To believe one is immune to persuasion is itself a vulnerability. The confident executive who scoffs at advertising may still be swayed by prestige branding. The scholar who disdains propaganda may nonetheless succumb to groupthink within academia. Resilience begins with acknowledging susceptibility, then cultivating awareness of context: *who benefits from this argument? what assumptions does it smuggle in? how does it make me feel, and why?* These questions transform the passive recipient of persuasion into an active evaluator.

The stakes are not only individual but collective. Democracies depend upon citizens who can distinguish rhetoric from reason, propaganda from principle. When large populations lack resilience, misinformation spreads unchecked, polarisation deepens, and civic trust erodes. Conversely, when individuals cultivate critical autonomy, they strengthen not only themselves but the fabric of public life. In this sense, building minds that can withstand persuasion is not a luxury but a civic necessity.

And yet, a lingering tension persists. Can a mind be trained to resist persuasion without losing the warmth of connection, the openness to inspiration, the willingness to be changed by genuine truth? Might the very defences we build against manipulation harden into barriers against empathy and growth? The challenge is delicate, and unresolved. Resilience asks us to become both shield and compass: able to ward off manipulation, yet able still to orient towards what is good and true. How to hold that balance, how to teach it without tipping into dogmatism or despair, remains one of the most urgent tasks of education today.

Chapter 5
Resilience in a Culture of Fragility

On a crisp October morning in 2014, Yale University issued an email urging students to report any offensive Halloween costumes. Within days, debate erupted across campus. Was the call for sensitivity a noble act of protection, or a dangerous drift towards over-sheltering young adults from the uncomfortable realities of free expression? The controversy grew into a national spectacle. Beneath the noise, however, it reflected a deeper paradox: in societies where safety is prized above all else, strength can wither. The harder we work to shield students from difficulty, the less capable they become of navigating it when it inevitably arrives.

This paradox of fragility is not confined to elite universities. It seeps into parenting, schooling, and corporate culture. Playground surfaces are softened, syllabi sanitised, and work environments meticulously managed to avoid "undue stress." The intent is compassionate, but the unintended outcome is stark: young people arrive in adulthood less prepared to weather setbacks, less resilient in the face of uncertainty, and more prone to interpret discomfort as catastrophe. Safety has been overprescribed, until what once built toughness now breeds brittleness.

Resilience, in its truest sense, is not the absence of strain but the capacity to recover and adapt when strain occurs. Neuroscientists speak of "stress inoculation": just as the immune system strengthens when exposed to small doses of a virus, so too does the brain grow more adaptive through manageable stress. Sports psychology echoes this truth: athletes improve not by avoiding exertion but by deliberately engaging with it, pushing past thresholds and then recovering. A student protected from all academic failure is like an athlete barred from training—comfortable in the short term, vulnerable in the long.

The irony is that many schools, while claiming to prepare students for real life, create conditions that amplify fragility. Failure is framed as final rather than formative. A poor exam score brands a student as incapable rather than offering data for improvement. The cultural message is clear: stumble once, and you may never stand again. Yet history, science, and common sense insist otherwise. Failure, reframed, is not identity but feedback—a signal pointing towards growth. Innovators, entrepreneurs, and artists know this instinctively: every misstep is a rehearsal for mastery. But until schools rewire their relationship with failure, students will continue to fear it rather than learn from it.

The antidote lies in habit. Resilience is not a lofty trait bestowed on the lucky few but a practice, cultivated through routine disciplines. Journaling reframes setbacks into patterns of progress. Reflection transforms stress into lessons. Rest and recovery—so often neglected in cultures of constant achievement—restore the very resources needed to try again. These habits, modest in themselves, accumulate into an armoury against fragility. They remind us that resilience is not merely a concept but a lived rhythm.

As this chapter unfolds, it will probe the paradox of fragility more deeply, examine stress as training ground, reconsider the place of failure, and highlight daily practices that harden not the heart but the spirit. The stakes are not trivial. A culture that overprotects its young risks producing adults unable to adapt in a volatile world. The question pressing upon us, then, is not whether adversity will come—it will—but whether we will have taught the next generation to meet it with fear or with strength. The answer may determine not just personal outcomes but the resilience of entire societies.

The Fragility Paradox

In the spring of 2017, several universities across the United States began erecting "safe spaces" designed to shield students from offensive language and controversial ideas. Rooms filled with beanbags, colouring books, and soothing music were offered as refuges from the intensity of campus debate. For some, this was hailed as enlightened care for student wellbeing. For others, it signalled a troubling shift: the suggestion that discomfort, rather than being a normal part of growth, was a threat to be avoided. The paradox was stark. The more institutions sought to protect students from challenge, the less equipped those students seemed to be when challenge inevitably arrived.

This is the fragility paradox at work: a culture that prizes safety to the extreme often generates precisely the opposite of what it intends. What is meant to cultivate resilience instead fosters dependency, avoidance, and vulnerability. The language of protection may be compassionate, but its logic can be corrosive. Just as a child shielded from germs develops a weaker immune system, so too does an overprotected student struggle to mount psychological defences against the inevitable adversities of adult life.

To grasp the depth of this paradox, it is worth considering how societies have historically understood resilience. For centuries, apprenticeships, rites of passage, and even playground hierarchies exposed young people to controlled doses of stress and competition. These experiences taught negotiation, endurance, and adaptation. In contrast, modern culture often treats stress as toxic by default. Parents smooth every bump in the road, teachers inflate grades to guard self-esteem, and policymakers equate safety with success. The result is a generation encouraged to expect smooth paths but left unprepared for the rough terrain of reality.

Psychology and neuroscience suggest that such overprotection rewires the brain in unhelpful ways. Stress, when moderate and manageable, activates neural pathways that strengthen memory, attention, and problem-solving. It is a form of cognitive weightlifting. Deprived of these opportunities, students miss the very conditions that foster adaptability. Instead of developing tolerance for frustration, they cultivate hypersensitivity to it. Their threshold for discomfort lowers, leaving them more—not less—susceptible to anxiety and despair.

Consider the case of school assessments. A test result once offered feedback, however imperfect, about where a student stood and how to improve. Increasingly, however, tests are softened or eliminated on the grounds that failure damages self-esteem. While the intent is to protect, the effect is to deny students practice in responding constructively to setbacks. The avoidance of failure inadvertently magnifies its terror. When these students later encounter rejection—be it from a job, a relationship, or a financial setback—they lack the psychological calluses that might have absorbed the blow.

Critics of this argument sometimes counter that exposure to stress risks harm, pointing to cases of bullying, burnout, or trauma. And indeed, uncontrolled or chronic stress is damaging. The fragility paradox is not an endorsement of cruelty or neglect. It is a call for balance: an acknowledgment that human beings grow stronger not in the absence of difficulty but in its measured presence. A muscle never used atrophies; a spirit never tested stagnates. The challenge is to design environments that introduce manageable risks and genuine responsibilities, rather than wrapping life in protective padding.

One sees this principle most vividly in sport. A runner builds endurance not by jogging within a comfort zone but by stretching the body to the edge of fatigue, then resting, then stretching again. Resilience in life follows a similar pattern. Small exposures to stress—delivering a speech, navigating a disagreement, handling a minor financial setback—act as training grounds for the greater adversities to come. Shield students from all such tests, and their adult lives become the true battlefield where untrained minds and hearts falter.

Yet society persists in equating protection with care. Helicopter parenting, litigation over playground accidents, and the proliferation of "trigger warnings" all arise from a belief that safeguarding students from every discomfort is the mark of progress. But the data tells another story: rising rates of anxiety, depression, and self-reported fragility among young adults. The paradox deepens. In striving to create a culture of safety, we have inadvertently sown a culture of fear.

The deeper philosophical question, then, is whether resilience can be taught without risk. Can one learn courage without ever facing fear? Can one develop persistence without ever encountering frustration? The evidence suggests not. Resilience, unlike information, cannot be passively acquired; it must be actively forged. The very attempt to bypass this process—to substitute comfort for challenge—is what fuels the fragility paradox.

The tension remains unresolved. Parents, educators, and policymakers want students to flourish, but they disagree profoundly on whether flourishing means removing obstacles or learning to overcome them. For the moment, overprotection still dominates. Yet reality, as it always does, will intervene. Economic instability, political upheaval, and personal loss will make their demands, indifferent to how well-padded a student's early years have been.

The question that follows is both urgent and unsettling: will we continue to mistake protection for preparation, or will we have the courage to let discomfort do its necessary work? In that choice lies the future resilience—or fragility—of the next generation.

Stress as a Training Ground

In 2010, researchers at the University at Buffalo published findings that startled parents and educators alike. People who had experienced a moderate number of adverse events—financial setbacks, failed relationships, health scares—reported higher levels of life satisfaction and resilience than those who had faced either very few difficulties or overwhelming trauma. The study's message was simple yet unsettling: too little stress may be just as harmful as too much. The human mind, like the body, needs weight to push against if it is to grow strong.

This notion runs counter to the dominant cultural instinct to shield children and young adults from hardship. Yet history, neuroscience, and sports psychology converge on the same truth: *controlled exposure to stress is not an obstacle to flourishing but a condition of it.* Just as no athlete builds strength by lifting feathers, no student cultivates adaptability by moving through life without resistance. Stress, within tolerable limits, is not poison—it is practice.

Modern neuroscience reveals why this is so. When a person confronts difficulty, the body's stress response releases cortisol and adrenaline, sharpening attention and mobilising energy. If the challenge is surmountable, the nervous system learns to regulate itself more efficiently, resetting faster each time. Neural pathways strengthen, enabling quicker recovery and a broader repertoire of coping strategies. In effect, the brain rehearses resilience. Without these rehearsals, the stress response system becomes maladaptive, either overreacting to trivial challenges or collapsing under genuine pressure.

Sports psychology has long embraced this principle, packaging it under the concept of "progressive overload." A runner increases mileage gradually; a weightlifter adds resistance in increments. Each small strain tears muscle fibres that then repair stronger. Applied to life, the metaphor is clear: students who confront and overcome modest difficulties—public speaking, academic setbacks, social conflicts—develop the emotional musculature to face larger trials. Remove all friction, and one produces fragility, not strength.

Examples abound in educational contexts. Consider the student whose teachers never allow deadlines to stand, extending them indefinitely in the name of compassion. At university or in the workplace, where extensions are rare, the same student finds routine demands unbearable. Contrast this with the peer who is held accountable, who learns to manage time under pressure, and who discovers that missed deadlines carry consequences but do not define identity. One emerges brittle, the other resilient. The difference is not innate talent but the presence—or absence—of structured stress.

Yet our cultural reflex often paints stress in uniformly negative tones. Rising rates of anxiety disorders and burnout make this fear understandable. But here lies the critical distinction: *toxic, chronic stress corrodes; acute, bounded stress educates.* It is the difference between drowning in a storm and learning to swim in a pool. Neuroscientist Bruce McEwen once described stress as a process that "sculpts the brain." The question is not whether stress should exist but how it is channelled.

This raises uncomfortable questions for institutions that prize comfort over challenge. What does it mean when universities provide "safe spaces" for controversial debates rather than equipping students to withstand uncomfortable ideas? What does it mean when parents intervene in every playground quarrel rather than letting children negotiate their own social hierarchies? In each case, the intention is kindness, yet the outcome is the deprivation of stress-training that future life will demand in abundance.

Philosophically, the issue touches on an ancient paradox. The Stoics taught that hardship is the forge of virtue; the Buddhists, that suffering is the teacher of wisdom. Modern science, far from contradicting these traditions, appears to confirm them. Adaptability, courage, and patience are not traits one is born with but qualities honed through friction. The question is not whether students will meet difficulty but whether they will have been prepared in advance to interpret it as a teacher rather than as a catastrophe.

The practice of deliberately seeking manageable discomfort is already common in elite contexts. Military training, for instance, simulates extreme stress not to break recruits but to inoculate them, so that when real danger arrives, their nervous systems are not paralysed by novelty. Athletes submit to drills designed to replicate pressure so that competition feels familiar. Yet in ordinary schooling, stress is increasingly stripped away, as if difficulty were an aberration rather than a crucible.

One can see the cost in workplaces flooded with graduates who are technically skilled but psychologically fragile. A single critical review can send them spiralling; a failed project can be misread as evidence of personal inadequacy rather than situational challenge. They were never taught that stress, properly understood, is data: an indicator that growth is occurring, that limits are being tested, that adaptation is under way.

And so the paradox persists. We fear stress because it hurts in the moment, forgetting that pain is often the sensation of growth in progress. We avoid challenge to preserve immediate comfort, overlooking that comfort itself can become a trap. Stress is not the enemy but the rehearsal, the sparring partner, the rehearsal room where resilience learns its lines.

The unresolved question is whether society is willing to recalibrate its relationship with stress. Can we design schools, families, and workplaces that expose young people to difficulty without overwhelming them, that use stress as a training ground rather than treating it as contamination? Until we answer, we risk producing students adept at avoiding stress rather than mastering it—precisely the opposite of what the future demands.

Failure as Feedback, Not Identity

In 1879, Thomas Edison was asked about his seemingly endless string of unsuccessful attempts to create a functioning light bulb. His reply has since become legend: "I have not failed. I've just found 10,000 ways that won't work." To many, this is a comforting platitude. But to Edison, it was not comfort—it was method. Each misstep was data. Each broken filament was information. Where most saw failure as defeat, he saw it as feedback.

This distinction between failure as identity and failure as iteration is more than semantics. It is the difference between paralysis and progress. Yet in most schools, the opposite lesson is taught: failure is permanent, and those who fail are marked. A low grade is not treated as a provisional measure of understanding but as a final verdict on intelligence. A failed exam is not a signal of where improvement is needed but a scarlet letter on a transcript. In this environment, students quickly internalise a dangerous equation: *to fail is to be a failure.*

Psychology has given this equation a name: fixed mindset. Carol Dweck's research demonstrated that children who view ability as innate and unchangeable interpret every setback as evidence of deficiency. They avoid challenges, fearing the possibility of further "proof" of inadequacy. In contrast, those with a growth mindset see setbacks as opportunities to learn. They tackle difficult problems not because they expect to succeed immediately, but because they expect to grow in the attempt. The irony is striking: the very metric meant to measure learning—grades—often ends up curtailing it.

Consider the classroom dynamic when a teacher returns marked exams. Heads bow, shoulders tighten, and the room divides silently into "winners" and "losers." Rarely is the feedback interrogated for patterns. Rarely is error seen as guidance. Instead, the grade eclipses the process. Contrast this with the world of design or entrepreneurship, where iteration is celebrated. A prototype that fails in testing is not discarded but refined. A start-up that pivots after a failed product launch is often admired for its agility. In these domains, failure is not a stigma but an ingredient of innovation.

Why, then, do schools cling to a model that equates error with shame? Partly because institutions prize efficiency. It is easier to rank and sort than to diagnose and develop. Partly because cultural narratives idolise the flawless genius, the prodigy who "just knew." We prefer the myth of Mozart composing symphonies at five to the reality of him labouring, revising, and being taught by his father. But perhaps the deeper reason is emotional: failure unsettles us. To embrace it as feedback requires humility, patience, and courage—all qualities harder to teach than the quadratic equation.

Neuroscience adds further nuance. Studies of learning reveal that the brain strengthens connections most effectively when errors are made and corrected. A 2018 study at Baycrest Health Sciences showed that making mistakes, far from derailing memory, can enhance retention when followed by correction. Error, in this sense, is not noise in the system—it is the system. To deny students the right to fail is to deny them the very mechanism by which expertise is built.

The cost of misframing failure extends beyond classrooms. Graduates who have been shielded from or punished harshly for mistakes often arrive in workplaces risk-averse and brittle. They avoid innovation, fearing embarrassment or reprimand. Yet the modern economy rewards those who can experiment, iterate, and recover. Silicon Valley codified this into a mantra—"fail fast, fail often"—not because failure is desirable in itself but because speed of learning is. The paradox is stark: the environments most hostile to failure (schools) are those charged with preparing students for environments where adaptability to failure is essential (the workplace).

There are, of course, dangers at the other extreme. To romanticise failure without consequence is reckless. Repeatedly making the same mistake without reflection is not resilience but negligence. The key lies in interpretation. Failure must be decoupled from identity and reattached to process. A failed exam should not brand a student incompetent, but highlight specific areas requiring attention. A lost debate should not silence a pupil but sharpen their reasoning. The narrative must shift from *you are inadequate* to *you are incomplete, and incompletion is the human condition.*

Philosophically, this reframing touches on deeper questions of identity and growth. The Stoics urged their students to treat adversity as a gymnasium for the soul. The Japanese concept of *kaizen*—continuous improvement—emphasises the small, daily corrections that compound into mastery. Even evolution itself is, in a sense, a story of failure: endless mutations that do not thrive, until one does. Nature does not treat these dead ends as shameful but as necessary experiments in progress.

Imagine if education mirrored this ethos. Imagine if students were taught to analyse their errors with the same rigour they apply to solving correct answers. Imagine if a failed science project was graded not solely on outcome but on the quality of reflection it produced. Failure would cease to be an endpoint and become what it truly is: information, rich with possibility.

The transformation is not merely academic. To reframe failure is to rewire courage. A student who learns that mistakes illuminate, rather than condemn, is more likely to take intellectual risks, to venture beyond the obvious, to innovate. And this is what the world most desperately requires: not perfect test-takers, but bold problem-solvers unafraid of stumbling on the way to discovery.

The open question remains: can our institutions, steeped in traditions of judgement and hierarchy, make peace with failure as a teacher? Or will they continue to trap students in a false binary of success or shame? The answer will determine whether future generations inherit classrooms that crush curiosity or cultivate resilience. And it will shape whether failure remains a sentence—or becomes the spark of progress.

The Practice of Resilient Habits

When Navy SEALs are asked what separates those who survive the brutal "Hell Week" of training from those who ring the bell of surrender, they rarely cite brute strength or natural talent. They point instead to discipline—small, repeated habits that keep the mind steady when the body screams to quit. The lesson is as relevant to students and professionals as it is to elite soldiers: resilience is not a heroic trait summoned in crisis, but a set of cultivated routines, practised long before adversity strikes.

Modern culture romanticises resilience as a dramatic comeback, a phoenix rising from ashes. But the science tells a quieter story. Neuroscience and psychology suggest that resilience is built incrementally, through consistent practices that stabilise mood, enhance self-awareness, and allow recovery. Journaling, structured reflection, and intentional rest are not quaint self-help suggestions—they are training regimens for the mind, akin to strength exercises for the body.

Take journaling. At first glance, it can appear indulgent, a relic of adolescent diaries or literary confessionals. Yet research consistently links expressive writing to reduced stress, stronger immune function, and improved cognitive clarity. The act of putting emotions and experiences into words forces the brain to order chaos, to transform the diffuse swirl of feeling into structured narrative. Psychologist James Pennebaker's seminal studies showed that individuals who wrote about difficult experiences for just 15 minutes a day experienced measurable improvements in both mental and physical health. In educational contexts, students who journal their setbacks often develop a more constructive relationship with failure, seeing it not as a verdict but as material for growth.

Reflection takes this one step further. It is not merely recording what happened but interrogating its meaning. Consider professional athletes who watch recordings of their games, not for nostalgia but to dissect errors and refine strategies. In the same way, structured reflection allows individuals to analyse their own decisions, identify biases, and adjust behaviours. In corporate settings, companies that integrate after-action reviews—a form of collective reflection—outperform those that simply move on to the next task. For students, reflective practice transforms exams, essays, or presentations from endpoints into feedback loops. Without reflection, experience risks becoming repetition; with it, experience becomes learning.

Then there is recovery. In a world that glorifies relentless hustle, deliberate rest is often mistaken for laziness. Yet resilience depends on cycles of strain and renewal. Neuroscience underscores this: the brain consolidates memory and problem-solving during rest, not in moments of overstimulation. Sports psychology offers a parallel. Athletes who train without recovery invite injury and burnout. Those who build recovery into their schedules—through sleep, nutrition, or mindfulness practices—perform not only harder but smarter. For students and professionals alike, resilience is not about pushing indefinitely, but about knowing when to pause, recharge, and return stronger.

Critics might dismiss such routines as luxuries available only to the privileged. But history suggests otherwise. The Stoics practised daily reflection to steel themselves against fortune's blows. Soldiers in trenches kept diaries not as literary projects but as survival tools. Monastics structured their lives around cycles of prayer, labour, and rest, understanding that clarity of mind required discipline of habit. These practices were not abstract ideals; they were lifelines.

At the same time, habits are double-edged. Just as positive routines can inoculate against stress, negative ones—doomscrolling, avoidance, overwork—can compound fragility. The challenge is intentionality: to choose habits that reinforce strength rather than erode it. In this sense, resilience is not about the grand gesture but about daily decisions. Will one spend ten minutes reflecting or ten minutes scrolling? Will one acknowledge the need for recovery or surrender to the cult of exhaustion?

There is also a philosophical dimension to resilient habits. They anchor identity in process rather than outcome. The act of journaling says: *my worth is not tied to today's success or failure, but to my willingness to engage with both honestly.* Reflection says: *I am a work in progress, and progress is meaningful in itself.* Recovery says: *I am finite, and to respect my limits is to preserve my capacity to contribute tomorrow.* These are not small admissions; they are radical counterweights to cultures that idolise constant achievement.

Seen this way, resilience ceases to be reactive and becomes proactive. It is no longer something we hope to summon in crisis but something we rehearse in daily life. The paradox is that habits which appear ordinary—writing a page, reviewing a day, taking an evening walk—are in fact extraordinary investments in future strength. They transform resilience from an abstract virtue into a lived practice.

The question is not whether individuals will face stress, failure, or crisis—they inevitably will. The question is whether, when those moments come, they will arrive empty-handed or equipped with routines that steady their minds and guide their recovery. Resilient habits are not ornaments of a well-ordered life; they are its infrastructure. And if cultivated deliberately, they can transform fragility into adaptability, and setbacks into the raw material of growth.

Chapter 6
Social Navigation Without Scripts

In the late 19th century, when Sigmund Freud first began to map the contours of human behaviour, his clinical notes reflected a world where face-to-face interaction dominated every aspect of life: families dined together nightly, neighbours conversed over fences, apprentices learnt directly from masters. Today, the average adolescent spends more time in mediated exchanges—likes, swipes, messages—than in unstructured, embodied conversation. The paradox is striking: never have we been more "connected," and yet never have so many struggled with the basic grammar of human connection.

Walk into a modern classroom or office and you may find students and young professionals fluent in coding languages, adept at navigating complex platforms, but uneasy when asked to interpret the flicker of doubt in a colleague's eyes or the subtle pause before someone says *yes*. Social interaction, once absorbed implicitly through community life, is now treated as if it were optional enrichment rather than core survival knowledge. Yet history suggests otherwise. Across centuries and cultures, the ability to read intentions, build alliances, and negotiate boundaries has determined who thrives and who falters—not only in politics or commerce, but in everyday human survival.

What makes this absence so consequential today is the speed at which social cues now determine opportunity. Psychologists estimate that first impressions form within milliseconds, influenced less by the words spoken than by posture, tone, and microexpression. A handshake too limp, a smile held too long, an email sent without sensitivity to hierarchy—all can subtly alter the trajectory of a career or a relationship. We might like to imagine ourselves as purely rational actors, but in truth we live and work in a world shaped by impressions, gestures, and the unspoken rules of interaction. Ignoring this dimension leaves students not neutral but vulnerable, manipulable in negotiations, and uncertain in collaboration.

This vulnerability is magnified in a globalised workplace. Teams no longer draw solely from local talent but from continents apart, shaped by distinct cultural scripts. A gesture of agreement in one culture may read as hesitation in another. A silence meant as respect can be misread as disengagement. The stakes are high: the ability to bridge ideological and cultural divides is not an optional virtue but the currency of modern leadership. To misinterpret signals is to risk mistrust, while to master them is to unlock collaboration across difference.

And yet, schools rarely treat social intelligence as teachable. Negotiation is left to chance. Persuasion is confused with manipulation. Setting boundaries is treated as a private challenge rather than a public skill. The irony is stark: students can analyse Shakespeare's sonnets for themes of power and influence, yet may graduate unable to decline an unreasonable request from a supervisor without guilt or self-sabotage. What we call "soft skills" are, in truth, the hardest skills to acquire without guidance, and the cost of their absence is paid in strained relationships, stalled careers, and eroded confidence.

To frame this chapter as a lament, however, would be to miss the opportunity. The science of human connection is no longer vague intuition—it is increasingly mapped by psychology, neuroscience, and communication research. We now know that trust can be cultivated through consistent signals, that negotiation follows patterns which can be taught, and that influence without manipulation rests on clarity rather than coercion. These insights dismantle the myth that social fluency is innate and show instead that it can be learned, practised, and refined with as much rigour as mathematics or science.

But here lies the tension: in a culture of templates and scripts, true social navigation cannot be reduced to formula. The point is not to hand students a set of rehearsed lines but to equip them with frameworks flexible enough to adapt in real time. To read a room not by following a checklist but by listening with precision. To negotiate not by mimicking hardball tactics but by understanding interests beneath positions. To persuade not by exploiting bias but by aligning truth with resonance.

The chapters that follow will explore this hidden curriculum of human connection—from decoding the power of first impressions to negotiating with fairness, from building bridges across difference to setting boundaries with confidence. At stake is nothing less than the ability to live and work with others without being dominated by them, and to lead without resorting to manipulation.

The question is pressing: in a century where algorithms mediate much of our speech, will we allow the art of human interaction to atrophy into awkwardness and exploitation? Or will we reassert it as a central skill of survival, as essential to a flourishing life as financial literacy or critical thinking? The answer, as this chapter suggests, may decide not only the fate of individual students but the health of our societies.

The Missing Lessons of Human Connection

A curious paradox defines modern life: the more time we spend connected through screens, the less adept we seem at navigating face-to-face encounters. A teenager today can maintain dozens of parallel conversations across platforms, yet may freeze when asked to introduce themselves in a room of strangers. Their digital fluency is unmatched, but their social reflexes—the subtle arts of eye contact, timing, and listening—are dulled. In a world overflowing with technological convenience, the ability to read another human being in real time, without the filter of a device, is quietly becoming a lost skill.

The consequences are not trivial. Evolution hardwired us for survival through cooperation: the capacity to detect trustworthiness in a glance, to sense belonging in a group, to discern threat in a raised voice. Strip away this literacy and young adults are left unmoored, vulnerable not to predators on the savannah but to the equally potent hazards of misunderstanding, manipulation, and isolation. If food, water, and shelter sustain the body, then social intelligence sustains the human psyche. To treat it as a "soft" skill, secondary to academic metrics, is to misunderstand its centrality to resilience, opportunity, and leadership.

Consider the workplace. A graduate may leave university armed with technical expertise, but when they step into a team meeting their trajectory depends less on raw knowledge than on whether colleagues perceive them as credible, approachable, or trustworthy. Research in organisational psychology consistently shows that social capital—the network of relationships and reputations—predicts career advancement as strongly as formal qualifications. The graduate who cannot read when to speak, when to hold back, or when to compromise is not simply at a disadvantage; they are navigating blind.

This erosion of interpersonal acuity is not accidental. Childhoods increasingly orchestrated around structured activities and digital entertainment leave little space for the unfiltered lessons of unmediated play: negotiating rules with peers, repairing ruptures after conflict, improvising alliances. These moments once functioned as laboratories for empathy, perspective-taking, and conflict resolution. Now, many students reach adulthood with academic fluency but without the instincts to decode unspoken cues, making them appear brittle in environments where adaptability is essential.

Yet to frame the problem as generational weakness is to miss the deeper structural shift. Our institutions prize the measurable: grades, test scores, credentials. Social intelligence resists quantification. It unfolds in the messy realm of nuance, subtlety, and the unsaid. Schools teach Shakespeare's soliloquies and statistical models but rarely teach students how to interpret a classmate's discomfort, or how to apologise with sincerity, or how to repair trust after a mistake. These absences send a silent message: that relational skills are peripheral, when in fact they are foundational.

The irony is stark. The very technologies that enable constant connection have also normalised a form of distance. Emojis and abbreviations flatten the complexity of expression. Algorithms curate echo chambers where misunderstandings are less likely to be corrected through dialogue. Students grow adept at projecting personas but less skilled at inhabiting the messy reality of authentic exchange. The performance of connection has replaced the practice of connection, and the cost is a generation less able to navigate the unpredictability of human relationships.

Yet social intelligence remains as vital as ever, and perhaps more so. It governs the success of a negotiation, the health of a marriage, the cohesion of a community. In geopolitics, leaders misreading cultural cues can ignite conflict. In business, a manager blind to team dynamics can squander talent. In education, a teacher who cannot sense when anxiety masquerades as disobedience may alienate rather than support. Each instance points to the same truth: the ability to *read* others is not an embellishment to human life but its compass.

This raises a provocative question: if we would never send students into the world without literacy in numbers or words, why do we send them out illiterate in human connection? The answer cannot be left to chance encounters or family circumstance, for the costs are too high. Anxiety and loneliness, now reaching epidemic proportions among young people, are not simply personal struggles but societal failures to equip individuals with the skills to navigate and nurture bonds.

Reframing social intelligence as a survival skill is not a rhetorical flourish but a recognition of its enduring importance. In an age defined by volatility—economic, cultural, technological—the ability to connect, to interpret, to respond with empathy and discernment, may prove the most stable foundation of all. The challenge, then, is whether we will continue to relegate these lessons to the margins, or whether we will have the courage to centre them, not as optional enrichment, but as indispensable preparation for life.

The question lingers: will we redefine education to include the quiet but powerful art of human connection, or will we allow students to master algorithms while remaining strangers to the people sitting beside them? The answer will shape not only the resilience of individuals but the health of our shared future.

The Science of First Impressions

Within seven seconds of meeting someone, our brains have already rendered a verdict. Friend or foe, competent or inept, trustworthy or suspect—these judgments form almost instantaneously, long before words can clarify intent. What is striking is not only the speed of this process but its stubbornness. Once lodged, first impressions tend to anchor our perceptions, shaping how we interpret every subsequent action. In courtrooms, in boardrooms, even on dates, what unfolds in those initial moments may weigh more heavily than years of subsequent evidence.

A classic illustration comes from the legal system. Studies have shown that jurors are more likely to trust testimony from witnesses who display calm, confident body language—even when the actual content of their words is identical to those delivered nervously. Similarly, candidates for leadership roles are often judged less by their CVs than by how they walk into a room, shake a hand, or hold a gaze. The unsettling truth is that the architecture of opportunity often rests on non-verbal cues we emit unconsciously. To understand the mechanics of these fleeting interactions is therefore not an indulgence but a necessity.

At the heart of first impressions lies the body. Evolution primed humans to scan posture, gestures, and expressions for signs of threat or alliance. A slouched stance may be interpreted as weakness; crossed arms as defensiveness; a smile as warmth. But nuance matters. A smile that never reaches the eyes is processed differently from one accompanied by subtle wrinkling around the corners—what psychologists call a Duchenne smile, often read as authentic joy. These distinctions are not the result of conscious calculation but of neural shortcuts refined over millennia. We feel them before we can articulate them.

Tone of voice plays an equally potent role. Researchers at Princeton University demonstrated that listeners can assess a stranger's trustworthiness, competence, or warmth within a single word spoken, based solely on vocal tone. Low, steady voices often signal authority, while high-pitched, erratic speech may be unconsciously coded as anxious or unreliable. Such snap judgments, though imperfect, shape whether doors open or close. In professional contexts, the way something is said can outweigh what is said.

Microexpressions—the fleeting, involuntary facial movements that flash for less than half a second—offer perhaps the most revealing data. Pioneered in the research of Paul Ekman, these expressions betray emotions people may wish to conceal: fear masked by bravado, contempt hiding beneath politeness. Skilled observers, whether interrogators or negotiators, often rely on these subtle cues to pierce through deception. Yet most people remain only dimly aware of them, responding to the "gut feeling" that something is off without knowing why.

Critically, while first impressions are natural, they are not infallible. Bias threads through the process, bending perceptions according to stereotypes, cultural assumptions, or personal insecurities. A confident posture in one culture may appear arrogant in another; direct eye contact in one context may be read as respectful, in another as aggressive. Thus, the science of first impressions is not merely about decoding signals but about recognising the lenses through which we view them. The danger lies not in forming impressions but in mistaking them for absolute truth.

This tension invites a deeper philosophical reflection: if human judgment is so quick and so fallible, what does it mean to cultivate fairness? On the one hand, we cannot eliminate our instinctive evaluations; they are part of our cognitive design. On the other, we can train ourselves to suspend overconfidence in those initial verdicts, to question whether our impressions reflect reality or bias. Just as emotional intelligence teaches us to interpret our feelings without being ruled by them, social intelligence requires us to interpret our impressions without being enslaved to them.

Practical implications abound. In business, leaders who understand the mechanics of first impressions can intentionally design environments that foster trust—arranging seating to reduce hierarchy, using warm vocal tones to diffuse tension, or modelling openness through body language. For individuals, awareness of how small signals are received can transform interactions: maintaining eye contact without staring, modulating tone to balance confidence with humility, practicing authenticity rather than performance. These are not manipulative tactics but deliberate acts of clarity, aligning inner intent with outward signal.

And yet, the fragility of these early judgments raises a sobering question: how many opportunities are foreclosed not by lack of talent but by misread signals in those first moments? How many collaborations never take root because two people walked away convinced, incorrectly, that the other was aloof, weak, or untrustworthy? If so much of our future is determined in seconds, the imperative is clear. We must not only master how we project ourselves but also cultivate humility in how we interpret others.

The science of first impressions, then, is not simply about decoding the silent language of body and tone; it is about recognising the power these impressions wield over the trajectories of lives and institutions. The challenge that remains is whether we can learn to harness this knowledge for fairness rather than distortion, for connection rather than division. For every handshake, every greeting, every glance carries within it the potential to open a door—or close it forever.

Collaboration in Diverse Groups

On a winter morning in 2008, the financial crisis brought together bankers, regulators, and politicians from across the globe. The decisions made in those tense meetings determined not just the survival of individual banks but the stability of entire economies. What became clear was not only the fragility of the financial system but the necessity—and difficulty—of collaboration across cultures, languages, and political ideologies. Some discussions broke down not over policy but because participants interpreted one another's signals through their own cultural lenses: what was meant as cautious pragmatism was read as weakness, what was intended as decisiveness came across as arrogance. The costs of misalignment were enormous, and yet they revealed a truth that extends far beyond economics: in a world knitted together by trade, technology, and migration, the ability to collaborate across difference is no longer a virtue. It is survival.

The paradox is stark. Never in history have human beings been so connected, and yet never has the potential for misunderstanding been greater. A workplace team today might consist of an engineer raised in Bangalore, a designer educated in Helsinki, a manager from São Paulo, and a client in New York—all collaborating in real time. Each brings not only technical expertise but a deeply rooted set of cultural assumptions about hierarchy, risk, time, and communication. If these differences are left unexamined, they breed frustration, mistrust, and failure. If harnessed with skill, they generate innovation that no homogeneous group could have imagined.

Behavioural science lends weight to this claim. Studies consistently show that diverse teams outperform uniform ones in problem-solving and creativity, provided they can manage the friction that diversity generates. Homogeneous groups may feel more comfortable—they nod along, share jokes, and reach consensus quickly. But comfort is not the same as effectiveness. Genuine collaboration requires the willingness to endure discomfort: the challenge of having one's assumptions questioned, the patience to listen through an accent, the humility to accept that one's preferred way of working is not universal.

A vivid example comes from global health initiatives. When Western doctors arrived in West Africa during the Ebola crisis, their biomedical protocols clashed with local burial rituals, which involved washing the bodies of the deceased—an act that tragically spread the virus. Progress came only when health workers began collaborating with community leaders, respecting cultural traditions while adapting them for safety. The breakthrough was not technological but relational: trust built through dialogue across profound cultural divides. The lesson is as applicable in boardrooms as in villages—without cultural attunement, even the best-designed solutions falter.

At its core, collaboration in diverse groups forces us to confront a philosophical tension: how can people remain rooted in their own identities while engaging openly with those of others? Too often, organisations veer to extremes. Some demand assimilation, flattening difference in the name of efficiency. Others romanticise diversity without equipping individuals with the tools to navigate it.

Both approaches fail. True collaboration requires a third path: an ethic of *cultural humility*. This means acknowledging that no single worldview holds all the answers, that every culture carries blind spots as well as insights, and that wisdom emerges through dialogue rather than dominance.

Power dynamics complicate this picture further. In theory, diverse voices are valued; in practice, louder or higher-status participants often dominate discussions. Consider how meetings unfold in many global corporations: those fluent in English often steer the agenda, while colleagues less confident in the lingua franca contribute less, even if their expertise is critical. Over time, this dynamic perpetuates inequality. Conscious facilitation—rotating leadership, structured turn-taking, or written input channels—can counteract such distortions, but only if organisations acknowledge that the playing field is not naturally level.

The psychology of belonging also plays a decisive role. Research shows that people are more willing to share bold or unconventional ideas when they feel psychologically safe—confident that they will not be ridiculed or penalised for speaking up. In diverse groups, this safety cannot be taken for granted. Microaggressions, unexamined stereotypes, or exclusionary humour can silently corrode trust. Creating resilience in collaboration therefore requires more than good intentions; it demands deliberate practices of inclusion, from how meetings are chaired to how feedback is delivered.

And yet, the payoff is immense. Consider the field of technology, where global collaboration has become the norm. Open-source projects thrive because contributors from wildly different backgrounds bring unique perspectives to the same codebase. What holds them together is not uniformity but shared norms: transparency, accountability, and the collective pursuit of better solutions. When diversity is coupled with such unifying principles, it becomes an engine of progress rather than a source of friction.

The larger question, however, stretches beyond practical strategies. It touches on how societies conceive of human difference itself. Is diversity a problem to be managed, or a resource to be cultivated? Are disagreements signs of dysfunction, or the raw material of innovation? The answers we choose will determine not only the health of our workplaces but the resilience of our democracies. For collaboration in diverse groups is not merely a professional skill; it is the cornerstone of civic life in an interdependent world.

The task ahead is therefore double: to sharpen the practical skills of cross-cultural navigation, and to cultivate the moral disposition to see others not as threats to be neutralised but as partners in a shared endeavour. The danger lies not in difference itself but in our failure to engage with it wisely. The unresolved question—the one each generation must answer anew—is whether we will retreat into enclaves of sameness or rise to the challenge of building together across divides. The stakes could not be higher, for in the end, the future will be written not by solitary voices but by the chorus we manage to compose.

Negotiation, Persuasion, and Boundaries

In the mid-1990s, Nelson Mandela, newly freed after twenty-seven years of imprisonment, sat down to negotiate the political future of South Africa with leaders who had once overseen his captivity. The balance of power was precarious; violence threatened to engulf the nation. Yet Mandela's approach was neither capitulation nor coercion. He combined firmness with empathy, signalling both a refusal to be dominated and a willingness to imagine a shared future. It was negotiation in its highest form: not a contest of wills, but a disciplined practice of drawing boundaries, recognising interests, and persuading adversaries towards a workable peace. Few contexts are so extreme, but the principle remains: human progress depends not on the absence of conflict, but on the skill with which we manage it.

Most people, however, are never taught how. Schools may train us in algebra or essay writing, but rarely in the art of saying *no* without alienating others, of seeking compromise without self-betrayal, or of persuading without manipulation. As a result, many enter adult life either too compliant—agreeing to commitments that drain them—or too combative, mistaking bluntness for strength. Both extremes are costly. Without frameworks for balanced negotiation, people burn out in personal relationships, suffer in workplaces, and stumble in civic life.

At its core, negotiation is not about winning but about aligning interests. The Harvard model of principled negotiation, now a cornerstone of conflict resolution, insists on separating people from problems, focusing on underlying interests rather than stated positions, and generating options for mutual gain. Consider a workplace dispute over limited resources: two departments each demand priority funding. A positional battle ("we must have it") leads to stalemate. A negotiation centred on interests ("we need to meet project deadlines" versus "we need to maintain safety standards") allows space for creative solutions—perhaps phased funding or shared tools—that protect both sides. The skill lies not in outmanoeuvring the other party but in widening the lens to reveal hidden commonalities.

Persuasion, by contrast, is often misunderstood as the art of pressure. Yet the most effective persuaders are not those who overwhelm with arguments but those who invite identification. Aristotle's triad—*logos*, *pathos*, and *ethos*—remains instructive. Rational evidence alone seldom shifts behaviour; it must be intertwined with credibility and emotional resonance. Modern psychology confirms this: the *elaboration likelihood model* shows that people are moved by both central routes (careful reasoning) and peripheral cues (trust, affinity, authority). A doctor persuading patients to adopt healthier habits succeeds not merely by citing statistics but by establishing rapport, showing care, and embodying the credibility of lived expertise.

The danger arises when persuasion becomes manipulation. Dark psychology exploits the same mechanisms—trust, emotion, authority—but bends them towards domination. From advertising that preys on insecurities to political propaganda that inflames fear, manipulation corrodes both trust and autonomy. The line between persuasion and manipulation is subtle but vital: persuasion respects the agency of the other, manipulation undermines it. To persuade ethically is to offer reasons others can accept freely, to shape choice without stripping it of authenticity.

Boundaries complete the triad. Without them, negotiation collapses into appeasement and persuasion into exploitation. Boundaries clarify not only what we want but what we will not accept. They are not walls but lines of clarity, enabling others to engage with us honestly. A young professional overwhelmed by unpaid overtime may fear that saying no will jeopardise their career. Yet research in organisational psychology shows the opposite: employees who assert clear boundaries are often more respected, seen as principled rather than expendable. The skill lies in articulation—declining firmly yet respectfully, offering alternatives where possible, and resisting the guilt that often shadows self-protection.

These three practices—negotiation, persuasion, and boundary-setting—interlock. A skilled negotiator knows when persuasion can soften rigid stances, when boundaries must be drawn to preserve integrity, and when compromise can be sought without self-erasure. Conversely, without boundaries, persuasion slips into flattery; without persuasion, boundaries become brittle ultimatums. Mastery requires an ongoing calibration of firmness and openness, reason and empathy.

The stakes are not merely personal. In a globalised, pluralistic world, the health of democracies themselves hinges on these capacities. Public debate is negotiation on a grand scale, persuasion tested in the marketplace of ideas, boundaries asserted between freedom and harm. When citizens lack these skills, societies fracture into polarisation: shouting replaces listening, manipulation eclipses dialogue. Teaching negotiation and persuasion as life skills is therefore not a luxury but a civic necessity.

The question that lingers is this: in a culture saturated with noise, where manipulation masquerades as persuasion and compromise is branded as weakness, can we still cultivate a generation capable of drawing clear boundaries, negotiating fair outcomes, and persuading with integrity? The answer will determine not only how we navigate our workplaces and relationships, but how we safeguard the very possibility of living together in difference.

Chapter 7
The Attention Economy and the Battle for Focus

In 2017, a leaked internal memo from a major social media company revealed something that many had long suspected but few had dared to state outright: the company was not merely competing with other platforms, but with *sleep itself.* Hours of rest, family dinners, silent walks—anything that drew users away from their screens was seen as a rival. The bluntness of the statement was shocking, but its logic was undeniable. In a world where advertising revenue depends on how long our eyes remain glued to glowing rectangles, the fiercest competition is for the finite minutes of human attention. Data may be harvested, clicks may be counted, but the true currency—the resource everyone is scrambling to control—is focus.

The paradox is that never before have human beings had so much access to knowledge, yet never before has it been so difficult to think clearly. The same devices that deliver instant access to libraries of information are engineered to fracture concentration into fragments. We are promised empowerment, but what we often inherit is exhaustion—an endless scroll of notifications, messages, and pings that leaves the mind buzzing but unfocused. The challenge is not simply technological; it is existential. If we lose the capacity to direct our attention, every other skill—creativity, resilience, empathy, critical thought—falters with it.

This chapter takes the reader into the heart of that struggle. It begins with the recognition that attention is not merely a neutral resource, but a contested one, deliberately targeted by industries that understand the fragility of human cognition. Drawing from cognitive psychology, we will see how apps and platforms hijack neural triggers: the dopamine spikes of variable rewards, the subtle manipulations of interface design, the social anxieties stoked by metrics of likes and shares. These are not incidental by-products; they are intentional strategies that turn distraction into profit.

From there, the lens widens. We will confront one of modern culture's most stubborn myths—that multitasking represents progress, a mark of sophistication and agility. The evidence tells a different story: multitasking degrades productivity, diminishes learning, and erodes memory. Far from equipping us to thrive in complexity, it leaves us scattered, dipping shallowly into many things while mastering none. To recover depth in thought and work requires a rehabilitation of what now feels radical: single-tasking, the deliberate immersion in one activity at a time.

Yet resistance is possible. The latter half of the chapter will map practices for training attention, drawing not on self-help platitudes but on evidence-backed strategies. Neuroscience and performance psychology converge on the same insight: sustained focus is a skill that can be cultivated. Through deliberate routines, structured environments, and habits that honour cognitive rhythms, we can carve out pockets of deep work even in a world designed to disrupt them. The aim is not to retreat from technology, but to reclaim agency within it.

The stakes are both personal and civilisational. On an individual level, the battle for focus determines whether one's life is lived reactively—shaped by algorithms and notifications—or intentionally, shaped by choice. On a collective level, it raises the question of whether societies can still sustain the kind of long-term thinking needed to address crises such as climate change, inequality, and technological ethics. Without attention, democracy itself is at risk, for manipulation thrives where critical focus withers.

To live well in the attention economy is to recognise that the greatest act of freedom may no longer be speech, but silence—the capacity to direct, hold, and protect our focus amid forces designed to fracture it. The question that remains is whether we can muster the discipline to reclaim this resource before it is fully colonised, and whether the next generation will inherit minds capable of depth in a world of noise.

Why Attention Is the New Currency

In the late 1990s, a start-up in Silicon Valley launched a radical experiment. Instead of charging users to access its services, it offered everything for free. Investors were puzzled. How could a company survive without selling products or subscriptions? The answer lay in a simple but transformative idea: *what they were really selling was not information, but the time and focus of their users.* Two decades later, this logic dominates the global economy. Platforms worth billions thrive not because of what they produce, but because of how effectively they capture, package, and auction the human gaze.

The paradox of our age is that we live in a world of abundance—information, entertainment, communication—yet experience scarcity more acutely than ever. Not scarcity of food or shelter for many in the developed world, but scarcity of attention. There are only twenty-four hours in a day, and only so many moments in which the mind can concentrate with depth. Attention is finite, fragile, and fiercely competed for. The result is that every ping of a notification, every headline designed to outrage, and every advertisement placed between YouTube videos is part of a vast, invisible marketplace where the currency is not money but focus.

This commodification of attention has far-reaching consequences, many of which are not immediately visible. Traditional economics measures wealth in terms of capital or labour. But if we shift the lens, we see that the most valuable companies of our time—Google, Meta, TikTok—derive their worth from the minutes we spend engaging with their platforms. The product is not the service; the product is *us*. The logic is elegant in its ruthlessness: harvest micro-slices of human attention, feed them into data-driven advertising systems, and sell influence to the highest bidder.

Understanding this shift is not just about exposing the manipulations of tech giants. It is about recognising that focus underpins every other human capacity. To learn a language, one must sustain concentration. To build a relationship, one must listen without distraction. To create, one must enter states of deep work that require uninterrupted immersion. In this sense, attention is not only a commodity but a foundation—the bedrock skill without which all others erode. When our attention is scattered, so too is our ability to reason, imagine, or connect.

Psychologists have long understood that attention functions as the gatekeeper of consciousness. William James, writing in the 19th century, described it as "the taking possession by the mind, in clear and vivid form, of one out of what seem several simultaneously possible objects." What James could not have foreseen was how this gatekeeper would be besieged in the digital era. Neuroscience has since shown that attention is closely linked to working memory and executive function—the very faculties that allow us to prioritise, plan, and act with intention. When attention is fragmented, cognitive performance declines; when it is cultivated, clarity and creativity emerge.

Consider the consequences in education. A student who cannot hold attention across a forty-minute lecture will struggle to extract meaning, no matter how intelligent they are. In the workplace, employees bombarded with emails and Slack messages every few minutes operate in a perpetual state of cognitive triage, rarely entering the deeper states of problem-solving required for innovation. And in public life, the erosion of sustained focus leaves citizens vulnerable to manipulation, as algorithms exploit momentary outrage to steer opinion and behaviour.

This reframing of attention as currency also raises unsettling ethical questions. If corporations monetise focus, who protects it? Unlike physical resources—forests, rivers, minerals—attention has no formal guardianship. Governments regulate pollution and taxation, yet the pollution of minds through distraction is treated as mere lifestyle choice. The responsibility is pushed onto individuals: turn off notifications, practise mindfulness, impose screen limits. These are useful strategies, but they miss the larger structural truth—that the entire economy is wired to monetise our wandering minds.

And yet, to despair would be to misunderstand the opportunity. If attention is a currency, then learning to invest it wisely may be one of the most empowering skills of the 21st century. Just as financial literacy equips us to manage money rather than be enslaved by it, attentional literacy can free us from compulsive distraction. To choose where to place one's focus is to reclaim sovereignty over one's life.

The question is how. Can we teach students not only to resist the lure of constant stimulation but to experience the richness of sustained focus? Can professionals learn to treat attention as a resource to be budgeted as carefully as time or money? Can societies imagine frameworks where attention is safeguarded as a collective good rather than strip-mined for advertising profit? These are no longer abstract concerns. They shape the texture of our daily lives, the quality of our institutions, and the future of our democracies.

Attention has become the rarest resource in an age of abundance. The challenge now is not merely to acknowledge its value, but to act as if it truly were a currency—as precious, as limited, and as worthy of protection as any natural or financial asset. Whether we can rise to this challenge will determine more than our productivity. It will shape who we are, and what we become, in a world that never stops competing for our gaze.

How Technology Hijacks Minds

One of the most chilling confessions to emerge from Silicon Valley in recent years came not from an ethicist but from a designer. "We don't build apps to help people," he admitted, "we build them to capture attention." The admission was not a slip of cynicism but a reflection of the design logic driving much of our digital world. The glowing screen in your pocket is less a neutral tool than a slot machine engineered for the brain, exploiting the very neural circuits that evolved to help our ancestors survive.

The paradox is stark. Technology promises liberation—faster communication, effortless access to information, seamless connection across continents. Yet, at the very moment it claims to free us, it ensnares us. What looks like convenience is often compulsion; what appears as choice is nudged, guided, and manipulated. The question is not whether our devices influence us, but how deeply they reach into the unconscious layers of our cognition.

At the heart of this manipulation is the brain's dopamine system. Neuroscience shows that dopamine is not a chemical of pleasure, as often mischaracterised, but of *anticipation.* It surges not when satisfaction is guaranteed, but when it is uncertain. This is why slot machines are addictive, why we compulsively check for new emails, and why a social media notification exerts a gravitational pull stronger than rational intention. Designers know this. Variable reward schedules—the unpredictable reinforcement of likes, comments, or streaks—mirror the psychology of gambling. Each swipe or tap becomes a bet, each refresh a roll of the dice.

The hijacking extends beyond reward. Consider the infinite scroll, a design now ubiquitous. Traditional media ended: the bottom of the page, the close of a programme, the credits of a film. Digital platforms abolished endings. The absence of natural stopping cues keeps the user in a state of suspended attention, much as casinos eliminate clocks and windows to blur the perception of time. What feels like casual browsing often amounts to hours lost, siphoned invisibly through micro-interactions designed for stickiness.

Then there is the exploitation of social instincts. Humans are exquisitely attuned to belonging and exclusion. A message left unread, a streak broken, a friend's highlight reel glowing with curated triumphs—these small signals tap into primal fears of being left out. Psychologists call it *FOMO*—fear of missing out—but that phrase trivialises a deeper phenomenon. Evolution wired us to monitor the tribe for threats and alliances. Platforms mimic this vigilance, pushing us into a constant state of comparison and anxiety. To log off feels not like disconnection from an app but like exile from a community.

Perhaps most insidious is the illusion of choice. We believe we scroll because we choose, yet algorithms decide what we see and when. They learn our triggers—what outrages us, what delights us, what keeps us scrolling just a little longer. These predictive systems are not neutral curators but profit-driven engines optimised for engagement, regardless of the emotional or societal cost. Outrage keeps eyes on screens longer than nuance; extremity spreads faster than moderation. Thus, our attention is pulled not toward what is true or enriching but toward what is sticky.

The consequences are not confined to wasted time. Cognitive psychology reveals that frequent interruptions erode working memory and diminish the brain's capacity for deep thought. Attention fragmented across dozens of micro-distractions becomes harder to reassemble into sustained concentration. This "cognitive switching penalty" is measurable: even brief diversions leave residues that reduce accuracy, productivity, and creativity. A generation raised on constant notifications risks losing the mental stamina required for scholarship, innovation, or meaningful dialogue.

Yet it would be simplistic to paint technology as a villain. The very mechanisms that hijack our minds can, when harnessed differently, support growth and learning. Educational platforms can use variable rewards to reinforce study habits. Fitness apps can leverage social accountability to promote health. The ethical line lies in intention: are these triggers deployed to serve the user, or to exploit them? This is where philosophy enters the conversation. If autonomy is the capacity to govern one's own attention, then technologies designed to override that autonomy are not neutral tools but political actors, shaping what we notice and what we neglect.

The deeper question is what kind of humans we become when attention itself is commodified. To be perpetually distracted is to live on the surface of life, never descending to the depths where meaning and originality are forged. The ability to choose focus, once assumed, is now contested. And if freedom begins with the sovereignty of the mind, what happens when that sovereignty is perpetually undermined?

The reality is that technology has learned to whisper to the brain in its own language—dopamine, uncertainty, fear of exclusion, craving for novelty. These whispers bypass reason and seep into instinct. The challenge is no longer to decide whether we will use technology, but to decide how to resist being used by it. The next frontier of literacy may not be in reading words or numbers, but in recognising when one's own mind is being manipulated.

That recognition, however, is only the beginning. The larger task is to imagine systems that respect attention rather than strip-mine it, to build cultures that value depth over distraction. Whether such a transformation is possible remains an open question. For now, the slot machine still glows in our pockets, and the roll of the dice is only ever a swipe away.

The Myth of Multitasking

In the 1990s, as personal computers infiltrated offices and homes, a seductive phrase entered the cultural bloodstream: *multitasking*. Borrowed from computing, it conjured an image of efficiency, of sleek productivity that allowed workers and students alike to do more with less time. Juggle an email, a spreadsheet, and a conversation simultaneously; handle three assignments while browsing the news and messaging a friend. To multitask was to keep pace with modernity, to prove oneself capable of matching the speed of the machines. Yet what sounded like mastery has revealed itself to be a profound illusion.

Neuroscience tells a very different story. The human brain cannot, in fact, attend fully to two demanding tasks at once. What we call multitasking is usually *task-switching*—a rapid toggling between activities that creates the illusion of simultaneity. Each switch carries a cognitive cost. Attention splinters, working memory falters, and errors multiply. Far from saving time, multitasking often extends it, as the brain requires several minutes to recover the depth of focus lost during each interruption. It is as if we imagine ourselves expert jugglers, when in reality we are merely dropping and catching in frantic sequence, never holding more than one ball at a time.

The costs are not merely theoretical. Consider the empirical evidence: psychologists at Stanford found that heavy media multitaskers were not only worse at filtering irrelevant information but also less able to manage their working memory and sustain attention. In essence, the very people who prided themselves on doing many things at once had trained their minds to be scattered. Another study from the University of London revealed that multitasking on cognitive tasks could lower IQ scores as much as losing a night's sleep. If sleep deprivation is now recognised as a public health concern, why not distraction?

The irony deepens when we examine environments that encourage multitasking. Classrooms with laptops, open-plan offices with constant notifications, households filled with the hum of multiple devices—all promote a culture where divided attention is normalised. Yet these are precisely the spaces where deep concentration is most needed. Students attempting to learn complex material while toggling between apps encode less information in long-term memory. Workers trying to solve problems amid pings and alerts make poorer decisions. In both cases, the myth of productivity cloaks a hidden tax: diminished learning and weaker judgment.

And yet, the cultural pressure to multitask persists. Employers equate busyness with value; students feel guilty if not layering study with entertainment; even leisure time is sliced into fragments of divided focus. Underneath this pressure lies a philosophy: that efficiency means compression, and that faster is always better. But what if the opposite were true? What if depth, slowness, and undivided focus yielded not only higher productivity but also richer satisfaction?

Philosophically, this is not merely about efficiency but about the shape of consciousness itself. To give attention fully is to inhabit the present, to allow thought to extend beyond the shallow. Fragmented attention, by contrast, breeds a life perpetually lived in halves—in which reading is interrupted by glances at the phone, meals are punctuated by notifications, and conversations become mere backdrops to digital chatter. What is lost is not only productivity but intimacy, creativity, and meaning. A distracted mind is not just inefficient; it is impoverished.

The cultural myth of multitasking also reveals a deeper misunderstanding of human worth. We valorise the person who appears constantly in motion, juggling multiple obligations, as though dignity were measured in speed and simultaneity. But machines multitask because they are incapable of thought; humans excel precisely because of their capacity for sustained attention, reflection, and synthesis. By aspiring to the machine, we risk abandoning the qualities that make us more than it.

There is, however, a counter-movement emerging. Thought leaders in technology and psychology alike call for a rehabilitation of single-tasking. Practices such as "deep work," popularised by Cal Newport, argue for carving out uninterrupted blocks of time in which the mind can achieve flow. Neuroscience supports this: brain imaging shows that focus recruits networks of neurons into synchronised activity, amplifying creativity and problem-solving. Such coherence is impossible when attention is continually scattered.

The practical implications are profound. To write well, one must write without distraction. To learn deeply, one must study without interruption. To listen fully, one must resist the lure of the phone vibrating in the pocket. Each of these acts of single-tasking is not merely a tactic but a reclaiming of autonomy over one's own attention. In a culture that prizes divided focus, choosing unity of attention becomes a quiet form of rebellion.

Still, the myth of multitasking will not vanish easily. It flatters our egos, it fits the pace of our technologies, it reassures us that we can somehow keep up with the flood of demands. Yet beneath that myth lies the truth that attention is finite, and that every act of division is an act of diminishment. The question, then, is whether we are willing to accept the limits of the mind—not as a weakness, but as a strength.

Perhaps the more radical challenge is not to ask how much we can do at once, but how deeply we can do one thing at a time. That question, more than any technological innovation, may determine whether we cultivate minds capable of wisdom, or simply scatter ourselves into fragments too small to matter.

Training for Deep Work

Imagine a violinist in a rehearsal hall. For three hours, she plays the same phrase again and again, her bow hand aching, her ears straining for nuance. To an outsider, this repetition looks monotonous, almost punishing. Yet within that focused immersion lies the making of mastery. The same principle applies to writers, coders, scientists, or entrepreneurs. The ability to direct attention deeply and sustain it for long stretches is not a luxury but a decisive advantage. It is, however, an ability increasingly rare in an environment designed to fracture concentration at every turn.

The paradox of our age is that we live surrounded by tools promising efficiency, yet those very tools scatter us. Notifications, feeds, and open tabs exploit the mind's vulnerability to novelty, drawing us towards shallow engagement. In contrast, deep work—the state of undistracted focus in which complex problems are solved, ideas are refined, and original contributions emerge—requires deliberate training. It is not innate talent, but a skill cultivated through discipline.

Cognitive psychology sheds light on why deep work feels difficult. The prefrontal cortex, responsible for executive control, tires quickly when forced to override impulses triggered by dopamine-driven cues. Every time a phone buzzes, the brain experiences a micro-surge of anticipation, which erodes the stamina needed for sustained focus. Neuroscientists liken this to muscle fatigue: just as untrained muscles fail under strain, untrained attention collapses under distraction. The encouraging insight is that, like muscles, attention can be strengthened through practice.

One proven practice is *time blocking*. Instead of drifting through tasks reactively, individuals allocate stretches of the day for uninterrupted focus. Research shows that even ninety minutes of concentrated work, when protected from interruptions, can yield breakthroughs that hours of fragmented effort cannot. For example, software developers at top-performing firms often schedule "no meeting" mornings to allow for uninterrupted coding, knowing that complex mental models cannot be reconstructed after constant disruptions.

Equally powerful is the cultivation of rituals that cue the brain into a state of immersion. Writers often sit at the same desk with the same mug of coffee; athletes lace their shoes in a precise order before training. These routines signal to the nervous system: now is the time to focus. Neuroscience confirms this effect: consistent contextual cues reduce the cognitive load required to enter flow, allowing the mind to bypass resistance more easily.

Another cornerstone is *embracing boredom*. In a culture of constant stimulation, the ability to tolerate stillness becomes a competitive edge. Studies from the University of Central Lancashire show that people allowed to daydream before tackling creative tasks generated more original ideas. By resisting the urge to fill every idle moment with scrolling, individuals give their minds space to incubate connections. In practice, this might mean leaving the phone behind during a walk or resisting the impulse to check messages in a queue. Boredom, counterintuitively, trains the mind to resist distraction and strengthens the capacity for depth.

Recovery is equally essential. Just as muscles grow during rest, cognitive capacity is restored through deliberate downtime. Sleep, breaks, and detachment from digital devices are not indulgences but prerequisites for deep work. Evidence from sleep research highlights that memory consolidation and creative insight often occur during non-linear rest periods, when the brain reorganises information below the surface of consciousness. High performers across disciplines—from elite athletes to Nobel-winning scientists—are often those who treat recovery as seriously as exertion.

Yet deep work is not only a matter of individual habits; it carries philosophical weight. To work deeply is to reclaim autonomy over one's mind, to resist being passively shaped by algorithms designed to monetise distraction. It is to assert that value lies not in the volume of tasks completed but in the depth of contribution made. In this sense, training for deep work is not only practical but ethical: it aligns one's use of attention with one's highest aims rather than surrendering it to the trivial.

The challenge is formidable. Few environments encourage sustained focus; many actively erode it. Offices valorise constant availability, schools often prioritise breadth over depth, and personal devices are engineered to captivate. Against this backdrop, choosing deep work requires intentional countercultural practice. It demands carving out sanctuaries of silence, defending them against interruption, and holding to them even when the world clamours for distraction.

But the reward is transformative. Those who master deep work not only achieve more; they experience life differently. To be immersed in demanding thought or creation is to enter a state where time flows differently, where satisfaction arises not from external validation but from the act itself. Deep work cultivates resilience, creativity, and meaning in equal measure.

The unresolved question, then, is whether we are willing to endure the discomfort it demands—the quiet hours, the unglamorous repetition, the refusal to fragment ourselves—in exchange for the clarity it yields. In an economy and culture competing for our every glance, the discipline to dwell deeply may be the most radical act of freedom available.

Chapter 8
Decision-Making Under Uncertainty

In 1962, the United States faced a decision that could have tipped the world into nuclear war. Reconnaissance photographs revealed Soviet missiles stationed in Cuba, a mere ninety miles from Florida. The intelligence was incomplete, the risks immeasurable, the stakes existential. President Kennedy and his advisors had no guarantee that their actions—whether military strike, blockade, or negotiation—would avert catastrophe. They had only fragments of information, hurriedly assembled probabilities, and the discipline to reason in uncertainty. The Cuban Missile Crisis remains a case study in the most difficult kind of decision-making: acting without knowing enough, but knowing one must act all the same.

Most of us will never face choices of that magnitude. Yet in quieter forms, uncertainty governs our lives. A student must choose a university without knowing what doors each will open. A professional weighs the security of a stable job against the gamble of a startup. A parent deliberates over medical advice that is hedged in probabilities rather than certainties. These moments reveal a striking contradiction: though schools train us to seek the "right" answer, life rarely presents one. Instead, it offers trade-offs, risks, and ambiguous signals, demanding not the comfort of certainty but the courage of judgement.

The paradox is that modern education, designed to prepare young people for the "real world," too often leaves them unready for the world as it is. By treating knowledge as a matter of correct responses to well-defined questions, institutions quietly suggest that clarity is the rule and ambiguity the exception. But beyond the classroom, ambiguity is not the exception; it is the constant. Markets shift, relationships evolve, health changes, technology upends expectations. To survive, let alone thrive, requires not the passive absorption of answers but the active cultivation of decision-making under uncertainty.

Behavioural science has shown us how ill-suited the human mind is for these conditions. We overestimate unlikely risks, underestimate slow-moving dangers, and cling to familiar narratives even when the evidence contradicts them. Our instinctive mental shortcuts—the heuristics that once kept our ancestors alive on the savannah—can betray us in the boardroom, the courtroom, or the household. Yet those same heuristics, refined by philosophy, statistics, and deliberate reflection, can become powerful tools. Probability thinking, Bayesian reasoning, and systems models transform uncertainty from paralysis into possibility.

The question is not whether risk can be eliminated—it cannot—but how it can be managed. Every meaningful decision involves a wager: we exchange the certainty of the present for a future imagined but not guaranteed. The entrepreneur betting on a product launch, the politician choosing a compromise, the individual deciding whether to speak or remain silent in a fraught moment—all are gamblers, though their chips are not coins but time, reputation, and opportunity. The discipline lies not in avoiding risk, but in weighing it.

This chapter examines the skills that make such weighing possible. It begins by dismantling the illusion of perfect knowledge, showing why incomplete information is the norm and how clinging to certainty is a liability. It then explores how to assess risks and rewards with the same clarity that actuaries bring to insurance or poker players bring to the table, applying these principles to the ordinary dilemmas of career and relationships. From there, it introduces mental models—philosophical heuristics and systemic frameworks—that offer scaffolding when facts are scarce and complexity is high. Finally, it considers the role of confidence: not bravado or rash certainty, but the quiet assurance that comes from disciplined reasoning, the willingness to act when the path ahead is still blurred.

To decide well under uncertainty is to cultivate a rare form of resilience. It demands humility—an awareness of what one cannot know—and courage—the resolve to move forward anyway. If there is a central irony, it is this: those who accept uncertainty as inescapable are best placed to navigate it. The alternative, waiting for clarity that never comes, is itself a decision—often the worst one available.

The question that lingers, then, is not whether we will face uncertainty, but whether we will be prepared to meet it. The world does not pause while we deliberate, nor does it reveal its secrets in full before we act. How, then, do we build minds capable of deciding amidst ambiguity—capable not only of surviving the unknown, but of shaping it? That is the challenge ahead.

Living With Incomplete Information

In the spring of 2020, world leaders were confronted with a novel virus spreading at alarming speed. Information was fragmented, data contradictory, projections speculative at best. Some governments locked down entire populations; others delayed, hoping for clarity that never fully arrived. Each choice carried profound costs. None were made with full knowledge. This moment of global uncertainty exposed a truth often ignored: most decisions that shape lives, economies, and futures are made with less than complete information.

Contrast this with the culture of the classroom, where students are taught to seek the single right answer, to distrust ambiguity, and to treat uncertainty as failure. The gap between school and life could not be wider. In one setting, ambiguity is punished with red ink; in the other, ambiguity is reality itself. Those trained only for certainty falter when certainty disappears.

The problem runs deeper than pedagogy. At its core lies a cultural discomfort with not knowing. In many classrooms, the rituals of testing and grading reinforce the idea that every problem is solvable if only one memorises enough rules. But in the world beyond the exam hall, rules collide, contexts shift, and information arrives late or not at all. A surgeon must decide whether to operate before all test results return. An investor must act with only partial visibility into markets. A citizen must vote with incomplete understanding of policy consequences. Life offers decisions more akin to chess against a hidden opponent than arithmetic on a clean blackboard.

Psychologists have long studied this phenomenon. The concept of *ambiguity tolerance*—the ability to remain functional and reasoned when knowledge is incomplete—emerges as a critical predictor of success in complex fields. Low ambiguity tolerance correlates with rigidity, anxiety, and rash decision-making. High tolerance, by contrast, supports adaptability, innovation, and resilience. Yet ambiguity tolerance is rarely cultivated in formal education. Instead, it is eroded by repeated reinforcement of the idea that ambiguity signals weakness or error.

Consider the story of the mathematician George Pólya, who famously advised his students not to fear uncertainty but to "guess and test, explore, and revise." For him, uncertainty was not an obstacle but the natural terrain of discovery. In contrast, a school culture that prizes only the polished solution robs students of the chance to wrestle with incomplete knowledge. It teaches them to perform certainty, rather than to think.

This tension between certainty and uncertainty echoes across philosophy. Socrates, with his relentless questions, embodied the humility of not-knowing as a path to wisdom. Descartes sought a foundation so certain that doubt itself could not undermine it. Modern decision theory accepts neither extreme: it embraces doubt as a permanent condition and develops tools—probability, statistics, models—to navigate it. The task is not to eliminate uncertainty but to reason within it.

Real-world case studies reveal the stakes. In aviation, pilots train rigorously to act when instruments fail, weather shifts, or communication is unclear. Their survival depends on decision-making under ambiguity, not on waiting for perfect information. In business, firms that hesitated for clarity during the rise of digital platforms were overtaken by more agile competitors willing to act on partial signals. In personal life, individuals who endlessly seek assurance before committing—to a relationship, a career move, a creative risk—often remain trapped in paralysis while opportunities pass.

The educational system's fixation on certainty has unintended consequences. Students become risk-averse, afraid to guess aloud in class, hesitant to explore ideas that lack immediate validation. Innovation suffers when fear of being "wrong" outweighs the courage to experiment. Worse, these habits persist into adulthood, where the absence of a clear rulebook leaves many unprepared to trust their judgement in conditions of uncertainty.

What would it mean to teach young people differently? Imagine classrooms where teachers openly admitted gaps in knowledge, modelling the humility of incomplete understanding. Where assessments rewarded not only the correct answer but also the quality of reasoning amidst uncertainty. Where students were encouraged to identify what they did not know and to make provisional decisions anyway. This would not undermine rigour; it would deepen it. For to think well under ambiguity requires sharper discipline than solving a textbook problem with a known outcome.

Living with incomplete information also demands a psychological shift. It requires comfort with *provisionality*—the understanding that today's decision may need to be revised in light of tomorrow's evidence. It requires courage to commit while knowing one might be wrong. And it requires resilience: the ability to recover, learn, and adapt when outcomes deviate from expectations. These qualities are not innate; they are cultivated through repeated exposure to situations where certainty is impossible.

Yet here lies the paradox. By protecting students from uncertainty, we deny them the very training that life demands. By insisting on right answers, we produce citizens and professionals ill-prepared for the messy reality of incomplete knowledge. Schools intend to prepare, but in this respect, they disarm.

The challenge, then, is not only pedagogical but cultural. Can we accept that ambiguity is not a defect to be corrected but the texture of human life? Can we value the thinker who navigates with partial maps as much as the one who recites complete formulas? To live with incomplete information is not to settle for ignorance. It is to face the world as it is: uncertain, shifting, unpredictable.

The more urgent question is whether we will reframe uncertainty as an enemy to defeat or as a condition to inhabit wisely. In that choice lies the difference between brittle minds and resilient ones—between citizens paralysed by the unexpected and citizens capable of steering through it. The answer cannot be given in advance; it must be lived into. And perhaps that is the lesson we most need to teach.

Risk and Reward in Everyday Life

A young professional stands at a crossroads. On one side lies the comfort of a steady job, predictable pay, and the quiet reassurance of stability. On the other side, a start-up beckons—uncertain hours, a high chance of failure, but also the possibility of extraordinary growth and freedom. The decision is not unlike a coin toss, except the coin is weighted in ways that are not immediately visible. What makes such dilemmas challenging is not the presence of risk itself, but the difficulty of calculating whether the potential reward justifies the gamble.

From the outside, it may appear irrational that some choose the start-up while others cling to security. Yet behind these choices lies a logic as old as human decision-making: weighing probabilities against outcomes, costs against gains, the near certain against the barely possible but transformative. Every major life decision—accepting a marriage proposal, moving abroad, investing in property—contains a similar calculus, whether or not we make it consciously.

The paradox is this: while people constantly engage with risk, most do so with little more than intuition. Schools train us to solve equations with fixed answers but rarely equip us with the probabilistic thinking needed to weigh uncertain futures. We crave certainty, yet the most consequential choices of life—those that determine careers, relationships, and legacies—offer only degrees of likelihood. Ignoring this reality leaves us vulnerable to either reckless leaps or paralysing hesitation.

Behavioural science has shown how poorly humans often handle risk. Consider lotteries, where millions wager against overwhelming odds, seduced by the vividness of the potential jackpot. By contrast, people underinvest in preventive health measures, though the probabilities clearly favour vaccination or regular screenings. This mismatch between perception and probability underscores a deeper challenge: the human mind tends to miscalculate both the likelihood and the value of outcomes, leaving us ill-prepared for everyday trade-offs.

Probability theory, however, offers more than cold mathematics; it provides a framework for clarity. Expected value—the principle that a choice should be judged not only by possible outcomes but by the likelihood of each—is particularly powerful. For instance, suppose a person considers leaving a secure position for a start-up where success carries the prospect of doubling their income but failure means starting over. If the probability of success is estimated at 30%, the expected value may rival or exceed the salary of the current job. This does not dictate the decision, but it reframes it: the risk is no longer a nebulous fear but a measurable component of rational choice.

Of course, life is not reducible to numbers alone. Emotional stakes complicate the arithmetic. A failed relationship does not merely "reset" to zero; it carries heartbreak, reputational scars, and lost time. A failed venture may yield invaluable lessons, networks, and resilience. These intangible consequences—both costs and benefits—must be factored into the decision, even if they resist precise quantification. What probability thinking does is not eliminate emotion but integrate it more deliberately into the analysis.

Take careers, for example. The graduate choosing between a law firm and a social enterprise is not only weighing salaries but also long-term satisfaction, identity, and purpose. The risk of burnout in one path may be higher; the chance of impact in another more uncertain but potentially more fulfilling. By considering both probability and payoff, the individual can avoid framing the decision as safe versus reckless, and instead see it as a balancing act between quantifiable and qualitative rewards.

In relationships, the logic is similar but often obscured. Deciding whether to commit, relocate for a partner, or end an unfulfilling bond involves trade-offs. The probability that a relationship will endure is unknowable in absolute terms, but people can consider indicators: shared values, conflict resolution styles, long-term compatibility. Here too, the expected value concept helps. Staying in a stagnant relationship may feel safer, but the potential reward of leaving—new opportunities for growth, self-discovery, healthier bonds—may outweigh the cost of short-term pain.

What complicates matters is that our perception of risk is coloured by biases. We overestimate vivid but rare dangers, like plane crashes, and underestimate mundane but lethal risks, like poor diet. We are prone to loss aversion, treating potential losses as more significant than equivalent gains. And we often frame decisions narrowly, asking, "What if this fails?" rather than, "What do I stand to gain if it succeeds, and how does that compare to the cost of failure?" Probability thinking offers a corrective, not by stripping decisions of humanity, but by providing a lens that counters the distortions of fear and wishful thinking.

Philosophically, risk is bound up with freedom. To act without risk is to abdicate agency, to let inertia make choices by default. Søren Kierkegaard wrote that anxiety is the dizziness of freedom, the price we pay for the possibility of choosing. In this sense, risk is not merely an obstacle but the very condition of a meaningful life. To love, to create, to lead—each requires stepping into uncertainty with eyes open. The question is not how to avoid risk, but how to bear it wisely.

The practical implication is that individuals must learn to become their own risk analysts. This does not mean living by spreadsheets, but cultivating habits of thought: asking what the realistic outcomes are, assigning rough probabilities, and honestly assessing the value of each. It means recognising when fear is inflating perceived risks, or when desire is exaggerating imagined rewards. And it means accepting that even the best-calculated decisions can go awry, because uncertainty is never eliminated, only managed.

In this light, risk and reward are not opposites but partners. Every reward worth pursuing requires a risk, and every risk worth taking must promise a reward. The skill lies in distinguishing between foolish gambles and thoughtful risks, between clinging to safety out of fear and embracing uncertainty with discipline.

The unresolved tension remains: how much uncertainty should one tolerate, and how much reward justifies the gamble? There is no universal answer. What probability thinking offers is not certainty but clarity—a framework to see trade-offs as they are rather than as we fear or fantasise them to be. And in that clarity lies the possibility of living not timidly, nor recklessly, but with deliberate courage.

Mental Models for Clarity

Imagine standing before a chessboard, pieces scattered, the clock ticking. The novice focuses on the move directly in front of them—how to protect a pawn or capture a knight. The grandmaster sees the board differently. Rather than evaluating each piece in isolation, they perceive patterns, anticipate cascading effects, and draw upon mental templates honed through years of practice. What looks like instinct is in fact the disciplined application of mental models—structured ways of seeing complexity and distilling it into clarity.

Life's decisions rarely come arranged like a chessboard, yet the principle holds. Most choices are messy, incomplete, and riddled with uncertainty. To act without a framework is to risk being swayed by surface impressions, emotions, or cognitive biases. Mental models serve as the scaffolding of clear thought: not rigid formulas, but durable heuristics that cut through noise and help us decide not with perfect foresight but with disciplined wisdom.

The notion of mental models owes as much to philosophy as to science. Systems thinking, probability, and ethics have each produced lenses through which to interpret the world. The Stoics urged a practice of distinguishing between what is within our control and what is not—a model of agency that remains profoundly relevant. Likewise, Bayesian reasoning invites us to update our beliefs in light of new evidence, rather than clinging to initial impressions. Each model is not an answer but a compass, offering direction when certainty is impossible.

Consider the map–territory distinction, articulated by Alfred Korzybski in the 1930s and later popularised by thinkers from general semantics to Warren Buffett. The idea is disarmingly simple: the representation of reality is not reality itself. Yet how often do we mistake economic forecasts, personality tests, or even news headlines for the full picture? Remembering that the map is not the territory inoculates us against overconfidence in models themselves; it reminds us that tools are aids, not oracles.

Another indispensable heuristic is second-order thinking. When making choices, humans tend to focus on immediate effects: a policy lowers taxes, a new technology creates jobs, a diet leads to weight loss. But systems do not stop at first-order outcomes. Lower taxes may also balloon deficits, technologies may displace as many workers as they employ, diets may cause long-term health consequences. Second-order thinking disciplines us to ask, "And then what?"—to follow the ripples rather than the splash.

Opportunity cost, a concept from economics, provides a further lens. Every decision is not merely a choice between doing and not doing, but between doing this and forgoing something else. Time spent on social media is not only consumed; it is stolen from reading, learning, resting, or creating. A job offer accepted means another one declined. By habitually invoking opportunity cost, individuals clarify what they are truly valuing in any trade-off, stripping away illusions of "having it all."

Mental models also function defensively, shielding us from manipulation. The principle of Occam's razor—preferring simpler explanations until complexity proves necessary—guards against conspiracy theories that weave elaborate plots where randomness suffices. The sunk cost fallacy model reminds us to abandon projects or relationships that no longer serve us, even when past investments tempt us to persist. These heuristics do not guarantee correctness, but they tilt the odds towards wiser choices by exposing hidden traps in our reasoning.

The beauty of mental models is their portability across domains. The same framework that helps an investor assess risk can guide a parent deciding on a school or a doctor evaluating treatment options. Take feedback loops, a concept from systems thinking. Positive feedback loops amplify changes—like social media algorithms feeding us more of what we click. Negative feedback loops stabilise systems—like the body sweating to regulate temperature. Recognising feedback loops enables us to understand not just isolated events but dynamic processes, whether in climate change, politics, or personal habits.

Philosophically, mental models provide not just clarity but humility. They remind us that every perspective is partial, every framework fallible. To think with models is not to become a prisoner of abstractions but to cultivate intellectual resilience. Just as a carpenter carries multiple tools, the wise decision-maker draws upon a repertoire of lenses—choosing the right model for the right situation, and knowing when to discard one that obscures rather than illuminates.

Yet models can conflict. Expected value may counsel one course of action, while ethical principles urge another. The reductive simplicity of a cost–benefit analysis may clash with the Stoic call to prioritise virtue over outcome. This tension is not a weakness but a feature: models are designed to provoke reflection, not automate decision-making. Clarity arises not from a single perfect lens, but from the interplay of many.

The challenge, then, is curation. In a world drowning in information, which heuristics deserve our limited attention? The answer lies in durability. The best models endure because they capture structural truths about human nature and systems. They are broad enough to apply across domains, yet precise enough to guide action. They simplify without distorting, illuminating patterns rather than trapping us in detail.

At its heart, adopting mental models is an act of intellectual self-defence. It is a refusal to stumble blindly through life's fog of uncertainty, and a commitment to building a toolkit that clarifies more than it confuses. Yet the question remains: which models will you choose to carry, and how will you train yourself to reach for them in moments of pressure? For clarity is not granted; it is practised. And the models we adopt shape not only the decisions we make, but the lives we ultimately lead.

The Confidence to Decide

In June 1940, as Nazi forces advanced through Europe, Winston Churchill faced a decision that would define not only his premiership but the fate of Britain itself: negotiate peace with Hitler, as many in his Cabinet urged, or commit the nation to fight on, alone if necessary. The information before him was incomplete, the risks catastrophic, the outcomes unknowable. Yet Churchill made the call. Not with arrogance, but with a disciplined trust in his reasoning and a willingness to bear the weight of uncertainty. Such moments remind us that decisiveness is not the absence of doubt but the ability to act in spite of it.

Our culture often confuses decisiveness with bravado—those who act quickly, loudly, or without hesitation are seen as leaders. But true confidence in decision-making is quieter, more deliberate. It rests not on the illusion of certainty but on a practised trust in one's reasoning process. To decide well is not to pretend we have perfect foresight, but to move forward with clarity about our principles, the evidence at hand, and the risks we are prepared to accept.

Hesitation has its virtues—reconsideration, reflection, caution—but indecision becomes paralysing when it stretches on indefinitely. We live in a world of proliferating options: endless career paths, countless newsfeeds, infinite choices on streaming platforms or dating apps. The abundance of choice can erode confidence, a phenomenon psychologists call "decision fatigue." The irony is stark: never before have we had so much freedom to choose, and never before have we been so anxious about whether we are choosing well.

Here the discipline of reasoning becomes essential. Confidence does not come from having all the answers but from practising a method. To define the problem clearly, weigh trade-offs honestly, consult durable heuristics such as opportunity cost or second-order thinking, and accept that no decision is immune to error—this is what builds the kind of confidence that endures beyond circumstances. Decisiveness emerges not as a flash of boldness but as a cultivated habit of clarity.

Consider the surgeon who must decide within minutes whether to operate, knowing that delay may cost a life yet haste may risk a misstep. Years of training, reflection, and repeated exposure to complexity allow her to act with confidence—not because she knows the outcome, but because she trusts the process that brought her to this point. In a less dramatic way, each of us faces similar crossroads: whether to change jobs, commit to a relationship, invest in a venture, or walk away. The stakes differ, but the need for disciplined trust in one's judgement is universal.

Confidence in decision-making also requires an embrace of accountability. To decide is to accept ownership of consequences, whether favourable or not. This distinguishes genuine decisiveness from reckless impulse. A gambler who risks everything on a hunch is not decisive but irresponsible. The leader who weighs costs, consults expertise, and then commits—even at personal risk—demonstrates the resilience that true confidence entails.

The paradox is that confidence often grows through error. Decisions that go awry teach us to refine our judgement, test our models, and recalibrate our expectations. Those who fear mistakes may cling to endless deliberation, but those who see failure as feedback learn to decide with increasing assurance. Confidence is not arrogance precisely because it is tempered by humility: an awareness that we will sometimes be wrong, yet a determination not to let fear of error immobilise us.

Cultural narratives about decisiveness vary. In some contexts, hesitation is seen as weakness, in others, as prudence. Yet across cultures, the leaders who earn respect are rarely those who avoided error altogether, but those who took responsibility, learned, and continued to act. Decisiveness, reframed in this way, is not about projecting certainty but about practising courage—the courage to move forward with imperfect information, guided by reason rather than impulse.

In a society saturated with noise, distraction, and second-guessing, the confidence to decide is more than a personal asset—it is a civic necessity. Democracies falter when citizens cannot weigh evidence and act. Organisations stagnate when teams circle indefinitely around options. Lives shrink when individuals avoid choice for fear of regret. To decide is to live deliberately, to resist being swept along by circumstance or the preferences of others.

And yet, the tension remains: how do we distinguish disciplined confidence from stubbornness, trust in reasoning from blind faith? This is the unresolved challenge every thoughtful decision-maker must face. For decisiveness is never final; each choice sets the stage for the next. The question is not whether we will always be right, but whether we will be ready—when the next moment of uncertainty arrives—to act with clarity, humility, and the courage to trust our minds.

Chapter 9
Redefining Success for the 21st Century

In the late 20th century, a script was handed to millions of young people across the developed world: study hard, secure a respected degree, land a prestigious job, work diligently, and you will ascend into the good life. For a while, that story seemed plausible. Yet as we step deeper into the 21st century, the script has begun to fray. Stable corporate careers dissolve under waves of restructuring. Entire industries are upended by automation or global competition. Graduates, once assured of upward mobility, now find themselves juggling temporary contracts, burdened by debt, or burning out in pursuit of titles that promise status but deliver exhaustion. The paradox is stark: never have the opportunities for individual advancement been more varied, and never has the sense of disorientation been greater.

If the 20th century defined success through visible markers—corner offices, gold watches, swelling bank accounts—the 21st is forcing a reckoning. What happens when the rewards those symbols promised are hollowed out by instability? What does it mean to succeed in a world where institutions can no longer guarantee security, and where the costs of blind ambition can be measured in mental health crises, fractured relationships, and lives reduced to perpetual busyness? We have inherited a model of success optimised for a different economy, a different rhythm of life. To cling to it today is to risk mistaking motion for meaning.

The critique is not merely economic but existential. Philosophy and psychology converge on a point the market rarely acknowledges: human beings crave more than wealth. We seek purpose, belonging, and freedom. Without these, prosperity feels shallow, no matter how large the pay cheque. Viktor Frankl argued that the will to meaning is more fundamental than the will to pleasure or power. Modern psychology echoes this: autonomy, mastery, and connectedness consistently predict well-being more reliably than salary figures alone. Yet cultural scripts continue to equate success with visible achievement, leaving many to feel like failures even when their lives are rich in less quantifiable ways.

This is not an argument against ambition, but for rebalancing it. A culture that glorifies relentless striving breeds fragility. We speak admiringly of resilience yet structure education and work in ways that normalise burnout. The pursuit of goals, whether in business or personal life, must contend with sustainability. How do we set ambitions that stretch us without breaking us? How do we measure success not only by milestones achieved but by the quality of the life lived along the way? These questions cut across generations, but they are especially acute for students and young professionals navigating landscapes their parents never imagined.

The 21st century demands a different kind of mindset: not one tethered to linear advancement, but one capable of adaptation. The successful individual of tomorrow will not be the one who clings to a single definition of achievement, but the one who can read shifting contexts, redefine goals, and align action with values. This does not trivialise financial stability—without it, autonomy and meaning remain precarious. Rather, it reframes wealth as one component of a larger equation, balanced with purpose and freedom.

The coming pages take this challenge seriously. They critique the outdated aspirations that still shape classrooms and family expectations. They explore how wealth, meaning, and autonomy intersect to form a more durable vision of success. They examine how ambition can be harnessed without sacrificing well-being, and they propose a mindset oriented not towards rigid achievement but towards resilience and choice. The aim is not to offer a tidy replacement for the broken script, but to prepare readers to write their own.

For the true measure of success in the 21st century may not be how far one climbs a single ladder, but how skilfully one navigates a shifting terrain—choosing, adapting, and thriving with integrity. The question that lingers, and with which we begin, is unsettling yet liberating: if the markers of success we were taught no longer serve us, what shall we put in their place?

The Trap of Outdated Aspirations

In 1969, a young graduate could walk into a bank, a law firm, or a government office and reasonably expect to spend the rest of their career there. The markers of success were clear: a secure salary, a steady climb up the professional ladder, and the prestige of belonging to a respected institution. Today, half a century later, the ground has shifted. A graduate may enter a tech start-up, only to see it vanish in a merger eighteen months later. A lawyer may find their role partially automated by algorithms. A banker may earn a six-figure salary but collapse under a workload that bleeds into every corner of personal life. The old aspirations—prestige jobs, high incomes, and institutional recognition—remain deeply ingrained in cultural imagination, yet their promise is increasingly hollow. The very symbols of success have become sources of instability, anxiety, and burnout.

The paradox is unsettling: society still teaches its children to chase a script that no longer exists. Schools celebrate university admissions to elite institutions as the pinnacle of achievement, parents beam at job titles that carry social weight, and peers measure themselves against salaries posted—often selectively—on social media. But beneath these glowing façades lie precarious contracts, disappearing pensions, and work cultures that reward sacrifice over sanity. To aspire to yesterday's success in today's economy is to run at full speed towards an outdated finish line.

Research on work satisfaction reveals the fracture lines. Surveys consistently show that many high-achieving professionals report disengagement, loneliness, and mental strain despite outward markers of success. Burnout is no longer confined to healthcare workers or teachers—it has become endemic in sectors once thought glamorous: law, finance, technology, academia. The irony is painful: individuals achieve precisely what they were told would bring stability and fulfilment, only to find it leaves them depleted. The prestige job becomes a gilded cage, the impressive salary a tether to unsustainable demands.

Part of the problem lies in how inherited models of success conflate *status* with *security*. In earlier generations, prestige often did bring stability. A doctor or civil servant could reasonably assume continuity of employment, housing affordability, and upward mobility. Today, globalisation, automation, and the gig economy have broken this link. High-prestige jobs can disappear overnight in corporate restructuring. Meanwhile, roles once dismissed as unremarkable—entrepreneurial ventures, freelance work, local businesses—sometimes offer more genuine autonomy and resilience. Yet culture continues to valorise the traditional ladder, leaving those who choose alternatives feeling as though they have failed.

The deeper issue, however, is philosophical. By defining success externally—in job titles, incomes, and accolades—we trap individuals in comparisons they cannot win. There will always be someone with a higher salary, a more prestigious position, a larger office. This treadmill breeds not contentment but chronic dissatisfaction, as psychologist Barry Schwartz observed in his work on the paradox of choice: the more options for status we see, the less secure we feel in our own standing. The inherited model of success does not merely clash with economic realities; it undermines psychological well-being by tying identity to perpetual competition.

Examples abound in the lived experience of students and young professionals. The medical student who pursues a speciality for prestige, only to find themselves disillusioned by years of overwork. The graduate who takes a consulting job for the salary, realising too late that they are trading autonomy for exhaustion. The entrepreneur who feels compelled to justify their path to sceptical relatives who cannot see beyond conventional benchmarks. In each case, outdated aspirations act less as guides and more as chains. They distort not only how people pursue careers, but how they measure their own worth.

None of this implies that ambition, wealth, or recognition are irrelevant. Financial security matters profoundly. Achievement can inspire growth and fuel contribution. The critique lies not in the pursuit of excellence, but in the *inheritance of rigid scripts* that no longer correspond to reality. Success must be redefined in ways that account for volatility, complexity, and the multidimensional nature of fulfilment. What use is a prestigious job if it corrodes health?

What value is a high salary if it eliminates the freedom to spend time with loved ones or pursue meaningful projects? These are not rhetorical questions—they are the dilemmas shaping modern life.

The trap of outdated aspirations is particularly dangerous because it masquerades as safety. Parents encourage children towards "secure" careers, blind to the fact that the very institutions they trust are under seismic strain. Schools elevate exam results and prestigious admissions, yet rarely prepare students to navigate instability. The result is a generation entering adulthood armed with inherited aspirations that function like maps to territories that no longer exist. They set out confidently, only to discover that the landscape has shifted beneath their feet.

To step out of this trap requires both courage and clarity. It means questioning assumptions passed down through family, culture, and education. It means recognising that prestige is not synonymous with resilience, and that income is not a perfect proxy for well-being. Most of all, it demands a willingness to measure success less by inherited scripts and more by alignment between values, choices, and lived experience. This does not make the path easier—indeed, it introduces new ambiguities—but it makes it real.

The unresolved question, which we must carry forward, is whether societies can reorient their definitions of success quickly enough to match the realities of the 21st century. If the old ladders lead only to burnout and disillusionment, what new structures, if any, will replace them? And can individuals, families, and institutions let go of cherished but crumbling ideals before another generation finds itself trapped in pursuits that no longer deliver what they promise?

Wealth, Meaning, and Freedom

In 1930, the economist John Maynard Keynes predicted that within a century, advances in technology and productivity would reduce the working week to fifteen hours. Human beings, he imagined, would be liberated from drudgery and free to pursue the good life: culture, companionship, intellectual exploration. His forecast was wrong in one crucial respect. Productivity soared, yet the working week for many has not shrunk; it has expanded in hidden ways, creeping into evenings, weekends, and holidays through the glow of a smartphone screen. The paradox is that even as societies grow richer, individuals often feel more constrained. More hours worked, more money earned, but less sense of freedom and fulfilment.

This tension raises an old but urgent question: what is wealth for? If it delivers neither happiness nor liberation, then its purpose must be reconsidered. Across cultures and eras, thinkers have wrestled with this problem. The Stoics warned against wealth as an idol, insisting that virtue was the only true good. Aristotle argued for a balance: enough material security to live well, but always subordinated to the pursuit of meaning. Modern psychology echoes these intuitions with data: money reliably increases life satisfaction up to a point—when basic needs and a margin of comfort are secured. Beyond that threshold, its marginal gains diminish, and the pursuit of more can erode the very conditions of contentment.

The challenge is not to denounce wealth but to situate it properly. Financial security remains indispensable. A person constantly anxious about rent, medical bills, or childcare cannot focus on higher aspirations. Poverty is not ennobling; it corrodes mental bandwidth and narrows horizons. But once survival and modest comfort are assured, the question shifts. What is one buying with the surplus? More often than not, it is not freedom but entanglement—longer commutes for larger houses, heavier debts for prestigious degrees, longer hours to maintain lifestyles that leave no time to enjoy them. Wealth can be either a foundation for flourishing or a trap of perpetual striving.

To move from security to fulfilment requires the integration of two other elements: meaning and freedom. Meaning provides orientation. It transforms effort into purpose, ensuring that life's inevitable struggles feel worthwhile. Viktor Frankl, reflecting on survival in concentration camps, argued that those who could find meaning—even in suffering—were more resilient than those who could not. In the modern workplace, employees who perceive their work as contributing to something larger than themselves report higher satisfaction and lower burnout, even when the pay is modest compared to peers in more lucrative but empty roles. Without meaning, wealth becomes sterile accumulation; with it, even modest resources can support a rich life.

Freedom, meanwhile, speaks to autonomy—the ability to shape one's days in alignment with values and desires. Research in self-determination theory highlights autonomy as a core psychological need, as vital as competence and relatedness. The banker who cannot leave their desk without checking messages is wealthier in salary but poorer in freedom than the teacher who finishes work by late afternoon and has evenings unencumbered. The freelancer with modest income but the power to choose projects may experience more genuine wealth than the executive whose calendar is dictated minute by minute by obligations. Real wealth is measured not just in currency, but in the degree to which one can direct one's own life.

The interplay of these three—wealth, meaning, and freedom—reveals their interdependence. Financial security without meaning breeds emptiness. Meaning without security can collapse under the stress of scarcity. Freedom without either risks becoming mere drift. But together, they form a durable triad. Consider the professional who earns enough to live comfortably, finds genuine purpose in mentoring others or building something of social value, and maintains control over when and how they work. Such a life may not impress every external observer, but it embodies resilience, contentment, and adaptability.

Cultural narratives, however, often pull in the opposite direction. The myth of endless accumulation insists that meaning and freedom will arrive once a certain level of wealth is achieved, as though they were accessories purchased with surplus income. Yet the evidence suggests the reverse: meaning and autonomy must be woven into life as guiding principles, shaping how wealth is earned and deployed. The individual who sacrifices all autonomy in the name of maximising income often finds themselves too depleted to pursue what matters once the money is secured. By contrast, those who align earning strategies with chosen values, even at the cost of lower salaries, often report deeper fulfilment.

The psychological literature on happiness reinforces this. Studies consistently show that experiential spending—on travel, learning, shared activities—brings more lasting satisfaction than material acquisition. Time affluence, the sense of having control over one's schedule, predicts well-being more strongly than income alone. These findings suggest that wealth should be seen less as an end and more as an instrument: a tool to purchase time, experiences, and autonomy. The true luxury is not the possession of goods, but the capacity to live in accordance with one's chosen priorities.

Philosophically, this reorientation echoes ancient wisdom. Epicurus argued that wealth is unnecessary for happiness once basic needs are met, and that friendship, reflection, and freedom from fear are the real sources of joy. The modern twist is that technology and globalisation have made these insights both more urgent and more difficult. The pull of consumer culture, fuelled by algorithmic persuasion, constantly tells us that the next purchase will bring fulfilment. Yet the dissonance is evident in the rising rates of anxiety, the sense of perpetual busyness, the erosion of community. Wealth without meaning or freedom leaves people rich in possessions but poor in spirit.

The future of success, then, must lie in balancing this triad. A society that equates success solely with income or prestige impoverishes itself, producing citizens who are financially comfortable but existentially restless. A culture that ignores financial security in favour of vague idealism risks exposing its members to unnecessary hardship. The art is integration: enough wealth to feel secure, enough meaning to feel alive, enough freedom to feel human.

And yet, the integration is fragile. Economic pressures, cultural scripts, and personal ambitions constantly threaten to tilt the balance. The unresolved challenge is how individuals and societies alike can resist the gravitational pull of outdated success models and design lives where wealth truly serves rather than rules. The question that remains is not whether financial security, purpose, and autonomy matter—they clearly do—but how we cultivate the wisdom to combine them, when each on its own can so easily lead us astray.

Balancing Ambition and Sustainability

In 2017, the World Health Organisation officially recognised burnout as an occupational phenomenon, describing it as the consequence of chronic workplace stress that has not been successfully managed. It was a striking admission: in societies that prize ambition, the very pursuit of success had become a public health crisis. Stories of overworked junior doctors collapsing after double shifts, of start-up founders sleeping under desks, of students burning out before graduation—all illustrate a culture where ambition has outpaced sustainability. The paradox is evident: drive, discipline, and high standards are celebrated as virtues, yet when taken to excess they corrode the very lives they are meant to elevate.

At the heart of this dilemma lies a tension as old as human striving: how does one reach for excellence without being consumed by the reaching? History offers countless cautionary tales. The Romantic poets wrote of flames that burned too brightly, extinguished by their own intensity. Modern psychology describes the same danger in clinical terms: overtraining syndrome in athletes, decision fatigue in executives, and emotional exhaustion in caregivers. Across domains, the pattern recurs: unchecked ambition produces diminishing returns, where each additional hour of effort yields less achievement and more damage.

The problem is not ambition itself. Ambition has driven scientific breakthroughs, artistic masterpieces, and social reform. To dismiss it would be to deny one of humanity's great engines of progress. The danger arises when ambition operates without balance—when the pursuit of more eclipses the capacity to sustain effort over time. Neuroscience sheds light here: chronic stress floods the body with cortisol, impairing memory, dampening creativity, and even reducing immune function. What feels like a relentless push towards goals may, at a biological level, be eroding the very faculties needed to achieve them.

Consider the phenomenon of overwork in Japan, encapsulated by the word *karōshi*—death by overwork. It is an extreme but telling example of ambition untempered by sustainability. Yet subtler versions play out daily in offices, laboratories, and classrooms around the world. The ambitious student who studies until 3 a.m. may pass the exam but undermine long-term retention. The executive who accepts every project may secure short-term recognition but jeopardise long-term effectiveness. Each case reveals the same principle: ambition, to be fruitful, must be yoked to rhythms of recovery and perspective.

Modern psychology and behavioural economics point to strategies that temper ambition with sustainability. One is the deliberate pacing of effort, akin to interval training in sport. Elite athletes do not simply push endlessly; they alternate intensity with rest, recognising that adaptation occurs in recovery. Likewise, professionals who intersperse deep work with genuine downtime are more productive across months and years than those who grind without pause. Another strategy is the adoption of *bounded ambition*: setting clear limits to prevent scope creep. This does not mean lowering standards but focusing ambition on chosen domains rather than scattering it across every opportunity.

Philosophy provides an additional lens. Aristotle distinguished between *pleonexia*—the insatiable desire for more—and *eudaimonia*—a flourishing life balanced by virtue. In modern terms, ambition untethered from moderation becomes pathological, while ambition aligned with sustainability leads to resilience. Stoic thinkers such as Seneca also warned against confusing busyness with achievement, reminding their readers that life is finite and misdirected effort is the greatest waste of all. These ancient cautions resonate powerfully in a world where emails never cease and metrics proliferate.

Case studies illustrate how balance can be achieved. Companies like Basecamp have institutionalised shorter working weeks, arguing that sustained creativity requires ample rest. Their results suggest that limiting hours can enhance, rather than diminish, output. Similarly, Scandinavian nations that prioritise work-life balance consistently rank high in both productivity and well-being. These examples challenge the notion that more hours equate to more success. They suggest instead that balance is not a luxury but a prerequisite for enduring achievement.

The personal level is equally revealing. Journals of high performers often record rituals of renewal: Beethoven's long daily walks, Maya Angelou's practice of working in short, intense bursts, followed by rest. Contemporary leaders increasingly speak of meditation, exercise, and digital sabbaths as essential—not peripheral—to effectiveness. The common thread is recognition that ambition cannot be sustained indefinitely without replenishment. Like a bow drawn too tightly, the mind and body eventually snap.

Yet a cultural contradiction persists. Young professionals are urged to "hustle," students are told that sleep is optional, and entrepreneurs are lionised for sacrifice. This narrative equates worth with relentless striving, making it difficult to practise restraint without feeling guilty. The challenge, then, is partly cultural: redefining success not as sheer volume of effort but as the capacity to pursue goals while preserving health, relationships, and perspective. Sustainability becomes not a compromise but a higher standard of ambition—ambition that lasts.

The unresolved question, of course, is how individuals and institutions can resist the gravitational pull of overwork in cultures that reward short-term gains. Can one be ambitious without being consumed? Can societies recalibrate to honour balance as much as achievement? The future of ambition may hinge not on how far we can push, but on whether we can learn to pause—long enough to recover, to reflect, and to ensure that the pursuit of success does not cost us the very lives we are striving to improve.

The Future-Proof Student Mindset

In 2020, when the world ground to a halt in the grip of a global pandemic, millions of students and professionals found themselves confronting the same unsettling truth: the rules had changed overnight. Degrees, career ladders, and carefully laid plans suddenly seemed fragile in the face of disruption. Some froze in uncertainty, waiting for the return of familiar structures. Others, however, adapted—learning new skills, building businesses online, reshaping careers, or simply adjusting their expectations without surrendering their sense of agency. What distinguished these groups was not talent alone, nor access to resources, but a quality harder to quantify: the ability to reframe uncertainty as a challenge rather than a catastrophe. That is the mindset that will define success in the twenty-first century.

The paradox of our time is stark. Never before have individuals had such abundant access to knowledge, tools, and opportunities; never before have those opportunities been so unstable, subject to the tremors of economic, technological, and cultural change. A profession admired today may be obsolete tomorrow; industries once thought immune to disruption dissolve within a decade. In such an environment, linear models of success—the kind that promise stability if one simply studies hard, secures a credential, and remains loyal to an employer—are relics. The contemporary challenge is not to climb a single ladder but to navigate shifting landscapes, improvising routes where no ladders exist.

This requires a reorientation of what we mean by "education". For centuries, schools have been organised around answers: correct ones, wrong ones, and the authority to decide between them. Yet the world outside the classroom offers far fewer certainties. Decisions about careers, investments, or even personal relationships are rarely accompanied by perfect information. To thrive in such contexts, students must cultivate not just knowledge but judgement—the capacity to weigh probabilities, to experiment, and to revise course in light of feedback. Adaptability is no longer peripheral; it is the essence of resilience.

Psychologists speak of *cognitive flexibility*—the ability to switch between different ways of thinking depending on the demands of the environment. Neuroscientific studies suggest that such flexibility can be strengthened through practice, much like a muscle. Exposure to novelty, engagement with diverse perspectives, and deliberate reflection all contribute to this adaptability. The future-proof student, therefore, is not the one who memorises most efficiently but the one who learns how to learn, and unlearn, and relearn when circumstances demand.

Case studies make this point tangible. Consider the rise of portfolio careers, where individuals juggle multiple roles—consultant, teacher, writer, entrepreneur—rather than a single linear path. What unites those who succeed is not mastery of one script but fluency in rewriting the script as needed. Similarly, in the technology sector, some of the most influential leaders began in fields far removed from coding or business—philosophy, literature, even archaeology. Their adaptability, not their conformity to predetermined paths, positioned them to seize opportunities when contexts shifted.

But adaptability alone is not enough. Without direction, it risks devolving into restlessness, a constant chasing of novelty without depth. Here, the synthesis of lessons from philosophy and psychology becomes essential. Success is not merely the ability to pivot but the capacity to pivot with purpose. Viktor Frankl, the psychiatrist who survived the concentration camps, argued that humans can endure almost any "how" if they possess a "why". In today's volatile world, purpose functions as a compass, orienting adaptability towards meaning rather than mere survival.

Equally vital is autonomy—the freedom to choose which battles to fight, which values to uphold, and which compromises to resist. Autonomy is not the same as independence; it is the ability to act in alignment with one's principles even within constraints. A future-proof mindset integrates ambition with self-discipline, creativity with discernment, flexibility with integrity. It recognises that the future cannot be controlled but can be navigated with intention.

Importantly, this mindset also embraces failure as part of the process. In fast-changing contexts, missteps are inevitable. What separates the resilient from the fragile is not whether they fail, but how they interpret failure: as identity-crushing defeat or as instructive feedback. The future-proof student sees each setback as data, each obstacle as an opportunity to refine strategies. This orientation demands emotional maturity as much as cognitive skill.

The danger, however, lies in misreading "future-proofing" as a demand for perpetual acceleration—always learning, always pivoting, never resting. That interpretation risks reproducing the very burnout it seeks to avoid. Sustainability remains central. The capacity to adapt is strengthened, not undermined, by periods of rest, reflection, and deliberate disengagement. Just as athletes build strength through cycles of exertion and recovery, so too do students and professionals build resilience through rhythms of focus and renewal.

The unresolved question remains: how do we prepare students not just to endure but to thrive in a century where change is the only constant? The answer is unlikely to be found in syllabi dense with facts destined to expire. It lies instead in cultivating dispositions: curiosity, humility, patience, and the courage to act without guarantees. To frame success not as the steady accumulation of accolades, but as the disciplined improvisation of a life that can absorb shocks, harness change, and still move with purpose.

The twenty-first century will not reward those who cling to certainty but those who can dance with uncertainty without losing their balance. To become future-proof, then, is not to build a fortress against change but to cultivate a mind and character capable of flourishing within it. The challenge—and the opportunity—is whether we can teach, model, and embody this mindset before the next disruption arrives.

About the Author

Evelyn Hawthorne writes about the skills school skips: clear thinking, financial fluency, and emotional literacy. Her work blends behavioral science with practical, plain-spoken tools that help students and parents make better choices in the real world. Over the past several years she has designed learning labs and workshops for classrooms and early-career programs, building usable habits around money, attention, and decision-making. She is the author of Everyday Signals and The Price of Forgetting, and is known for turning dense research into frameworks people can apply the same day. Evelyn's guiding belief is simple: a good education teaches you what to think about; a great education teaches you how to think—and how to live with judgment, curiosity, and steadiness.

www.ingramcontent.com/pod-product-compliance
Lightning Source LLC
Chambersburg PA
CBHW031351230926
51848CB00002B/478
* 9 7 8 9 3 7 1 7 7 7 7 7 3 *